Bluff &Vine

a literary review

Issue One
Fall 2017

Founding Editors: Alex Andrasik & Bethany Snyder
Consulting Editors: Sarah Thompson & R.W. Webb
Art Consultant: Doug Fleet

Cover art by Brenda Guidone.
Artwork courtesy of SkylArc Studio.
Arwork may not be copied without permission.

ISBN-13: 978-1979408257
ISBN-10: 1979408254

Printed in the United States of America.

Submission guidelines at
bluffandvine.com

Contents

A Note from the Editors

Welcome to our new, ongoing literary magazine. Not to be presumptuous, but we suspect that we have a lot in common: a love of moving literature; a desire to support local arts, and above all, a deep love for the beauty, history, and people that make up the Keuka Lake region. All of these factors drew us to launch this project, which aims to tap the wellspring of talent inspired by the Crooked Lake and its surroundings. In so doing, we have tried to capture, in both fiction and nonfiction, what makes this place so unique and special.

As writers, we love words and the ways we can play with them to make meaning. Thus our title: *bluff*, for the geologic feature that dominates our landscape, but also for its intriguingly dual meanings, both frank honesty and semantic trickery—a perfect distillation of the writer's craft; and *vine*, emblematic of the noble crop that has shaped so much local commerce and culture, but which also evokes the transport of knowledge and lore—as in, *I heard it through the grapevine*. We hope our humble offering lives up to the promise we've embedded in its name.

Our partnership with the Arc of Yates art studio, SkylArc, is reason for excitement and pride. From day one, we knew that we wanted to highlight the work of these talented individuals who so enrich our communities. We hope that the pieces we've included in this edition bring further exposure and recognition to the incredible art that they produce.

Good literature seeks to expose the breadth of human experience, from family-friendly to more adult themes; the coming stories fall all along that spectrum. We're confident in their literary merit, and invite you to explore the shape and depth of the Keuka Lake community that they expose.

Finally, be sure to visit us online at *bluffandvine.com* to view the artwork featured in this volume in beautiful color. There you will also find information on which pieces are for sale, and how you can purchase them.

Alex Andrasik & Bethany Snyder
Founding Editors

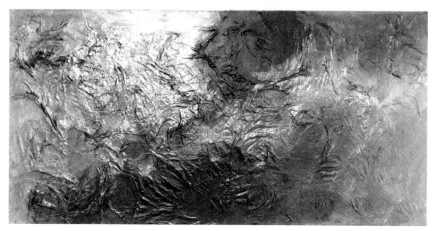

John Tomion

The Night the Wind Blew
Merrill Laura (Brown) Race

The house at 225 Clinton Street in Penn Yan where my sisters and I grew up was a home of many wonderful childhood memories. As kids, we loved being outside, playing hopscotch on the sidewalk just beyond the hedge, gathering horse chestnuts from Ogden's front yard across the street, and playing games on the old tree stump in the front yard. That stump was all that was left of a beautiful oak tree that came down during a violent storm when we were very young. None of us remember the storm. But Bonnie, the oldest (who was almost seven years old at the time of the storm), can remember that tree with its canopy of colorful leaves, one of many that lined the edges of Clinton Street before the storm. Our parents and grandparents, however, remembered vividly that night long ago, when Penn Yan and the Finger Lakes region of Central New York were slapped hard by Hurricane Hazel.

Dad always claimed they didn't know the storm was coming, but local newspaper accounts said the Civil Defense system had been activated early that Friday morning, October 15, 1954. Our area was supposed to get the tail end of Hurricane Hazel. Meteorologists expected Hazel to lose power going north of Florida, but the storm intensified and came ashore around Calabash, North Carolina, early that Friday morning as a Category 4 hurricane with sustained winds of 130 miles per hour and sped north.

The weather service predicted heavy rain for our area that night and into the next day. The Civil Defense system was enacted to take care of any possible flooding. Like our Dad, most folks believed the forecast was predicting nothing more than a rain event.

Mom wanted to go down to the Methodist Church to practice the organ after dinner that evening. She was an outstanding pianist, but playing the organ was different, and she needed to practice. Finding time to do so was difficult with three young children, so when our dad, an insurance/real estate agent, said he had a meeting with a client across town that evening, they came up with a plan where he'd drop her off at the church to practice on his way to his meeting. They enlisted our grandmother to babysit us girls at our house.

It was raining when Mom and Dad left the house and headed down Clinton Street toward the church. It was Friday night, and all the businesses downtown were open as usual. People were coming and going, ignoring the pouring rain as they went about their typical Friday night shopping. Dad dropped Mom off at the church, and said he'd be back to pick her up after his meeting.

By midday, Hazel became extratropical, but never lost power. The storm was plowing its way north at 55 miles per hour, with sustained winds of 75 miles per hour and gusts over 100—knocking out power, downing trees, and flooding creeks and rivers. The storm was over central Pennsylvania around 8 p.m. when it ran into a cold front that began pulling it slightly to the west.

Mom was pounding out the final notes to a hymn when she heard a low howling noise. She stopped and listened. It was coming from the bell tower, and it sounded like a banshee. She realized instantly that the storm was taking on a new personality. Whether driven by fear or a strong maternal instinct to reach us kids, she wasn't about to wait for Dad to pick her up. She immediately shut down the organ, flipped off the lights, and headed for home on foot.

It was almost nine o'clock when Mom left the church. The lights of downtown were still blazing when she blew around the corner onto Clinton Street. Sheets of rain slapped her in the back as the powerful southwesterly wind pushed her up the street. She could hear the roar of Jacob's Creek as she crossed the bridge, struggling to keep from being knocked over by the ferocious wind. Colorful leaves ripped from the trees swirled around her like confetti from a ticker tape parade as she crossed Benham Street.

Suddenly there was a crack, followed by a flash of light, as a large tree branch took out the electric cable over her head. Mom began to run. She splashed through puddles of water in front of Barone's grocery store, then leaped over the railroad tracks. After dodging a trash can that rolled at her as she sped past Ayers Dairy, she raced up the hill towards home. The big oak tree in the front yard, still loaded with colorful leaves, swayed back and forth as she pushed her way up the front steps into the dark house.

Our grandmother had brought us kids downstairs into the middle living room for safety. Power had just gone out. After finding the flashlight and lighting a few candles, we all hunkered down to wait out the storm. Suddenly, there was a loud crash. Mom and our grandmother jumped to their feet to investigate. The dining room door, which was tucked under the porch roof on the west side of the house and rarely used, had blown open. Rain was spraying all over the dining room, especially on Mom's beloved dining room table. Our grandmother said the wind was so powerful that it took both her and Mom to close the door and lock it.

Dad arrived home shortly thereafter. He said he'd gone back to the church to pick up Mom, but realized she'd already left. He attempted to head home up Clinton Street, but couldn't due to the downed trees and power cables. He turned around and went back to Main Street, then up Elm Street to Hamilton Street to get home. He bounded through the kitchen door just as Mom and our grandmother were cleaning up the mess in the dining room.

The eye of Hurricane Hazel crossed over New York State lines around nine o'clock that night, just west of the Genesee River. It was still packing Catagory 1 force winds, with gusts of 90 miles per hour. The storm's most powerful winds hit Penn Yan about 9:05 p.m. According to the *Geneva Daily Times* of October 16, 1954, "barns, trees, power cables, communication lines, and brick chimneys constitute the major casualties in Yates County today as a result of the visit of Hurricane Hazel Friday night." The storm lashed the area until 10:30 p.m. In Penn Yan, traffic was blocked on Clinton, Court, and Liberty Streets, where telephone lines and electric power cables were downed by fallen trees and limbs. The traffic light at North Avenue and Main Street was knocked down by winds, causing an electrical display before police and workmen arrived on the scene. Along Keuka Lake, boats were missing and docks were damaged from high waves kicked up by the ferocious winds. The worst part of the storm hit just as stores were closing after Friday night shopping hours, leaving motorists the difficult task of driving home in the wind and heavy rain.

By midnight, Hurricane Hazel centered over downtown Toronto and the Brampton area, where it merged with the cold front and stalled out, still producing 40 mile per hour sustained winds, and dropping eight inches of rain. The devastation was equivalent to the destruction caused by Hurricane Agnes to the Elmira/Corning area in 1972. Hazel slowly pushed northward, and died out over James Bay five days later.

We woke the next morning to the sound of chain saws. It was then we kids learned of the loss of our beautiful oak tree in the front yard. The storm had twisted off the tree trunk about half way up, and laid it across Clinton Street into the front yard of the Gurtha Pratt home.

Hurricane Hazel has gone down in history as the most destructive and costly storm of 1954. The storm left close to 400 people dead in Haiti, and over 90 in the United States and Canada. The storm removed all traces of civilization on the immediate waterfront between the North Carolina state line and Cape Fear; it practically annihilated every pier for 170 miles along the coast. Most of all, Hurricane Hazel brought long-lasting memories to a population that has rarely experienced the fury of a hurricane.

Story taken from the book
The House on Clinton Street, The Memories and Reflections of the Brown Sisters.

Matt Dunham

This Light is Here
P.T. Sweeney

She said her name was Christine, and I didn't want to argue.
That is the sort of thing, after all, that people tend to know about
themselves. Before they know most anything about the world and their
place in it, people typically know their names.

"Christine," I said aloud, wanting to hear it again, to check it
against what I thought was right about her and me and this gathering
of friends and strangers up on a hill in the dark. "Why don't I
remember you?"

"I guess… because... you forgot me," she said through a smirk.

"I remember a girl named Elizabeth. I think you were her. Or are her."

"Maybe you dreamed up this Elizabeth. Is Elizabeth your dream girl?" She was teasing. What I couldn't exactly see on her face in the flicker-flash of the bonfire, I could hear in the melody of her words and sense from how all her attention was now aimed my way. Before, she had been scanning the crowd of thirty or forty others wandering in and out of the cabin and around the fire, around the keg, through the dance of conversation. She had been looking into the dark to see who she could see, who could see her, and I suppose I had been, too. Now, it was her, and it was me, and the simple thrill of a summer night that might never bother to end.

"But you remember me."

"Yup," she said. "Seventh grade, eighth grade. I totally remember you. I don't think I ever really talked to you, but we sat in some of the same classes. And we knew some of the same people."

I sighed. I shook my head. I smiled. "Christine."

"Still Christine."

"Not Elizabeth."

"Not ever."

She was smiling then, too, I was sure. A sly smile on a sly face. Witty. That's what she was. Witty and pretty. Pretty and witty. Oh, I'd had a lot of beer.

I wish I could remember what else she'd said. I listened. I know that I listened. And she talked about how she'd lived here just for a few years, when she was eleven and twelve, how this was where her grandmother had lived, and how her mom had brought her here after her parents split and how she would come back summers and how she loved the lake and how Jessica was her cousin and how, yes, in case I was wondering, Jessica was still mad that I hadn't asked her to junior prom, and how she went to school now in Rochester and had changed majors to biology and *maybe* she was thinking about medical school but probably not. I remember that, all of that, and I remember how she would stop what she was saying whenever a Tom Petty song would come on to announce, "I love this song," and then go back to speaking all those casually frenetic words that I wish to God I could remember better.

I don't know how I had found her up there. It was the type of gathering where you needed to get up close before you'd know who was who. You heard voices and saw shapes in the summer night. A gesture could give someone away. Your ear might catch something familiar. A laugh—a laugh was sometimes the easiest way to recognize someone in that kind of dark you get in the country when the moon is off doing something else and you're happily far from every other bothersome source of light. Somehow, though, I had ended up talking to this girl near the fire, infatuated by her easy charm and the cascade of dark hair, infuriated by her insistence that she was not Elizabeth. She would later accuse me of having invented the whole Elizabeth business as some ruse to strike up a conversation with her, that I had probably approached countless other unsuspecting young women over the years with "that pathetic Elizabeth plot of yours."

I wasn't particularly interested in being anyone's boyfriend. What sensible twenty-year-old is thinking about that sort of entanglement? But here was this Christine, materialized out of some shared but unremembered past, suddenly and unshakably in my present. The charm of her, the thrill of her voice, these were things that could be indulged in the alternative universe of a summer night atop Bluff Point with friends and music and plenty of mediocre beer, up there where the breezes shift from warm to cool to cold, and you're that age, and you can't imagine how anything that isn't right there in front of you could possibly matter even one little bit. But there was a morning and a next day and a next week, too, and there still was Christine, and the hair and the smile and the phone calls and the walks and the laughter and endless conversations on a dock, our feet in the water. On a summer night, something as sure as tomorrow becomes impossible to imagine.

The tomorrows accumulated, though, without our realizing it, and summer was done. I was downstate. She was in Rochester. And hundreds of miles had put themselves between us. That should have been the point where the daily contact became occasional and then sporadic, and then that would be it. But she didn't want us to fall victim to summer cliché, and, somehow, neither did I. We talked on the phone, and I would visit her, she would visit me, and there we were, staring love in the face.

"You're going to need to get a second job just to afford gas, you know. This thing, all by itself, is probably supporting an entire village somewhere in the Mideast."

We were slipping through a snowy Rochester night to get pizza at her favorite place, which had suddenly also become my favorite place. Christine was not a big fan of the SUV that I drove then. This kind, generous, giant-hearted young woman had reserved all the hate in her heart for my Xterra. *The Xtrerrible gas mileage*, she'd say. *It's Xterrible for Mother Earth.*

"Is it too soon to think about next summer?" I asked her, needing to know if there was a chance we'd have another magical lake experience.

"You are thinking summer? *You?*"

"Me."

"Thinking ahead… planning. You? I don't know what to say about that, young sir." There was another of those megawatt smiles burning through the night. I didn't need to see it to know it was there.

"It's okay to be impressed," I suggested. "But... have you thought about it? I mean, is there a chance we could have that kinda summer again?"

"That summer? No. I don't think that summer could be had again. That was perfect because it was unexpected. So *that* summer can't ever happen again, but maybe some other kind of summer is possible."

I parked a block past the restaurant, and turned to face her. "I want us to be able to see each other every day again. I hate not seeing you all the time." The words sounded stupid to me, even as I spoke them. It was embarrassing to hear myself, but there was a desperateness to this moment, and I felt sure that her life and my life had intersected entirely by accident and now it was up to us to make sure that nothing else would be left to chance. "Let's figure out a way. You and me and Keuka and as much of summer as we can grab. Let's do it."

The talkative Christine sat there, looking at me, quiet and unreadable. It was a few seconds, probably, but time fell into the silence. "Have you ever noticed how in the afternoon up on the Bluff, the clouds come in? Big, beautiful, puffy clouds." She was speaking in a voice that was clear, but it was tired, too. She sounded dreamy, the way she did when we would talk on the phone late at night, when we desperately needed sleep but we talked a little while longer and then a little while longer than that. "They don't really block out the sun, even though there are so many of them. It's really, I don't know, really interesting to me, those clouds, how they zoom in, and, if you're up on the Bluff, and you stand still you can feel them coming in over your head. And they're up there, where clouds are supposed to be, but they seem so close. You know what I mean? It's like they're right *there*. It's so amazing to me. And it's something I don't see or notice anywhere else. Just up on the Bluff. It's like the whole sky is right there, so freaking close, and all you need to do is reach up and… *touch* it."

Her mind would work in this way, and she could pull the epic out of the ordinary. She was not like me, not like anyone I ever knew. She was Christine, and I, well, I was helpless. She was talking about clouds and the sky and the power of things that moved her, but I didn't know how any of that answered the important questions about whether we would ever be back there.

It was a few weeks later that she told about the internship: a summer in Atlanta, some classes, some lab experience, the kind of stuff that would get her a head start on grad school. "A great, great opportunity," she whispered over the phone, holding back her enthusiasm, aware that enthusiasm was a weapon that she didn't want to be wielding.

"It does sound great," I told her. It was my duty, I could tell, to let her know that she ought to be excited. She was holding back, I guess, as a way to balance the disappointment she hadn't prepared me for. Here we were, at our first real point of crisis, lifting each other up, talking about what a great thing it was, how she needed to go, how, of course, we would be fine, this would be no big deal for us, and it was great for her. So great.

"I didn't want to say anything till I knew for sure I'd get it. It was a competitive thing, and I didn't actually expect I would get accepted."

"You're smart, Christine. They need you."

"You're not mad?"

"I can't be mad."

"Yes, you can," she pleaded. "We won't see each other much—or at all—for the whole summer."

"You want me to be mad?"

"Maybe a little."

"Okay. Then I will be, a little bit. For, like, five minutes a day, every day, all summer. How's that?"

"That'll be perfect." She exhaled into a laugh.

"What about you? You gonna think about me when you're down there curing diseases or whatever?"

"Maybe a little."

"So, we'll be all right? The *us* thing, that's still gonna be a thing?"

"Depends on if you go meeting any cute girls at the lake this summer."

"I probably won't."

"I know how you are out there, kid. Saw it for myself. That sneaky charm."

"Yeah," I said, slumping to the floor, my back against the cold concrete wall. "That actually worked out for me last summer, didn't it?"

"Kinda did," she said.

"Probably would only work one time though."

"I hope so."

&

That summer in the Finger Lakes without Christine was not the nightmare I expected. It was fun, truth be told. But all the fun I had seemed set to a lower volume, as if something muffled the full enjoyment. Friends and family and drinking and camping and concerts at the Shell—it was all just fine. But it wasn't special. It was just a summer.

Christine's great opportunity turned out to be all she hoped it would be, and plenty more. Medical research became the thing she wanted to do and could do. That time in Atlanta ignited the spark for who she would become over the next few years in a master's program in Buffalo and as a research assistant in Baltimore. And the thing we'd stumbled into that summer at the lake faded one horrible winter when the distance became too much for us both. But then, it came back. And it was stronger, and it was too much to ignore. On a scorching summer afternoon on Bluff Point, under those clouds that she loved so much, we decided it would be a good idea to get married.

I found a job in the federal bureaucracy, and Christine went on researching communicable diseases, sure that she and her colleagues were on to something big. We set up in a townhouse in the Maryland suburbs, found time to travel abroad a couple of times, and to hike the ridges of the Shenandoah.

"It's a good life, isn't it?" she said as we sat overlooking a valley view that went seemed too fantastical to really be out there.

I agreed, and I remember turning my head just enough to see how she was seeing all this, knowing that she always saw more and felt more. I made a habit of doing this, because whatever we did would reflect off her, and be better because of her. Sometimes she would notice me looking, and that would break the spell, and she would feign annoyance and maybe slap my arm and tell me to stop being such a dork.

"I'm glad we came up here," I said. "Even though that trail was way harder than I expected."

"Worth it," she declared, and, looking around at all that was spread out before us. I knew she was right. She was right about a lot of things. "I think we need to look at that map again, though. If we're going to take that other loop, we're going to need to be sure it takes us where we think it takes us."

"You don't want to get lost out here?"

"No. No, I do not," she said.

"I don't know. Could be fun."

She glanced over at me, dropping her chin so that her eyes emerged over the top of her sunglasses. "You have a strange idea of fun, mister. Plus, we don't have enough water with us to go and get lost this many miles from civilization."

"Tell you what, if we get lost I'll go back to the car and get that other jug of water."

I thought this might be enough to get me one of those smacks, but

I was out of luck. It was just the eyes, the shining hazel truth of who we had become. "Let's get out of here alive, okay? We have important things to do."

"Maybe you do."

She shook her head, and then reached out to put her hand on mine and pull it to her abdomen. "*We* do. *All* of us."

And so there I was, the next spring, burping a shockingly beautiful little lump we called Clarisa, a phone to my ear. "Mark, I just don't know if it's gonna work. I mean, you've been a great boss, but, I don't know. Even with this flex arrangement and that, I... I just don't know if I can keep up a full-time schedule."

I had a perfectly dull job evaluating applications for federal grants, and I knew that someone needed to do that work to keep the country running. I also knew that just about anyone could do that work. It was in no way rewarding or interesting. It was a job I did in an office I went to. I loved hearing Christine talk about the things she did all day. A second glass of wine after dinner, and she'd go on about the progress being made on this research project or that, the absolute devotion she had to her work. It was terrific, the thrill she took in it, but I would spend my entire commute home some days trying to think of one scrap of interesting thing to talk about, should she ask how things were going for me in the service of our Uncle Sam.

It was a job I could quit, and so I did. Paying someone to take care of Clarisa all day while I did the monotonous things I did, that made no sense. "So very modern of us," Christine would say of this stay-at-home dad bargain we'd struck. Caring for an infant was a challenge, but it was not a burden. I liked most of it. I felt like I was accomplishing something, one feeding at a time, one balancing act on the way to first steps. This was parenting, and it had its rewards.

Plus, it allowed Christine to thrive in a career that mattered to her and to the wider world. It was a new concept of manliness, and at times it was awkward. My father, as proud as he was being a grandfather, seemed to have no idea how to talk to me.

"Hurry up and cure something already," I'd tell Christine when she'd ask if I was okay with my role in things. "Then I can tell people that all these diapers I've been changing contributed something to all of humankind."

"I couldn't do it without you," she would say, generously and repeatedly over those years. She appreciated my sacrifice, and I loved her all the more for it. We would bicker or argue so infrequently that I wondered if we were really married.

All the good, it was too good, because who gets all that love and kindness and patience and joy? No one. At least not us. Because then came the worried doctors, and the biopsies, and the goddamned chemo, and then all the glimmer fading from eyes that had never been anything but pure light and hope.

Clarisa was tired the day I took her to an open field on the Bluff. She ran a bit, and she tried to climb one of the giant round bales of hay. Then she sat on the ground, arranging the folds of her summer dress. I smiled at her, because smiling into her gentle face became a way of fending off the grinding grief that she and I felt working away inside us all day and all night. "Did you know it was just down this road a ways that I first got to know your mom?"

She looked at me, and then around us in that wide, open space. She seemed to want to see it, the exact place where her path had begun.

"Right up here," I told her. "One night a long time ago."

"It's nice up here," she said.

"Yeah, it sure is. Your mom, she loved it here. She loved it so much."

I think Clarisa nodded then, or maybe that's just how I remember it. That acknowledgement, if it wasn't real, well, I want it to be.

"You think I can get up on that one?" she asked, her arm pointing at a bale that was just as big as the one she'd tried to climb earlier.

"Maybe," I said. "Try it."

And so I stood there on legs that wanted to give out, and I watched her run hard and slow across that ground, arms out to each side, pushing away any obstacle that might try to thwart her journey. I watched, and I smiled, and I felt brave enough to weep into that warm afternoon.

If I could have stopped my mind from churning, I might be able to list of all the things I was no longer equipped to do. Would it be possible to name all the ways that death had disarmed me? I'd like to know, I think, what these things were, or, failing that, whether those things were even knowable. Just how had I changed, and who was this person I inhabited, this form that had dropped to its knees in the dirt. Did he know me, the me before I stopped being me? Did he know who I would never become?

The thing I could do now, the *one* thing, was look to up into the clouds. I could do that, with a hand and with hope, at least I could reach, and put a little part of me up into that faraway nearness, up there, because, if nothing else, this was this, and here still was the sky.

George Catroneo

Fishing With Dad On Keuka Lake
Butch Burris

I was twelve when we moved from Corning to Penn Yan; it was 1966. Dad bought a cottage just four miles out on the East Lake Road. Dad loved to fish for trout. My brother Jim and I loved to water ski and sail our Sunfish sailboat. At that age, we used the sailboat like most people would use a car; it was transportation to whatever touched Keuka Lake. They were wonderful days. Waterskiing and sailing were always fun, but now, looking back, the very best times were spent with Dad in his little aluminum fishing boat.

Dad used a Seth Green rig. Not the modern ones you see today with mechanical downriggers. Dad's was a wooden box about eighteen inches square, with cotton line coiled up in it. He would put heavy lead weights on it, and every so many feet, a leader would trail from it with either a shiny silver spoon or a saw belly minnow attached at its end. Holding the cotton line in his bare hand, Dad would let it go to the bottom and then raise it up just a little. My brother and I took turns rowing the boat.

I can still smell the clean lake smell and hear the cherry bombs scaring birds in the vineyards on quiet mornings. There was a serene beauty in the pale gray mist hanging over the hills. Dad's voice rings in my ears even now. "You see that tree over there, boys? Keep the stern right on that tree and row, boys." That's how we knew we were on the line he wanted to fish. Dad had the lake mapped out in his mind. He caught big lake trout that way, and we ate well from the bounty of Keuka Lake.

Dad had suffered a battle with polio in Italy during World War II. His left leg and right arm were affected by the disease. I never saw Dad as crippled. I only saw a man who had the challenge of two limbs that would not work as well as they should, and him meeting that challenge with confidence and courage. I remember being surprised to see grown men walking normally.

One time while fishing, I told Dad I didn't think it was fair that he did all the fishing and Jim and I labored at rowing. Great father that he was, Dad immediately agreed with me, and volunteered to let me fish while he rowed the boat. With the challenge of his two damaged limbs, it was not easy for him to move around in the boat, but for me, he cheerfully hoisted himself into the center seat and instructed me on how to operate the Seth Green rig. I listened carefully to him, and dreamed of that whale-sized lake trout that I would bring in.

"Now hold the line in your hand and work it, Butch," he said. "You have to let it touch the bottom so you know it's all the way down, then pull up a little so it doesn't drag. Then keep lifting it up and letting it down with a rhythm so that it makes the spoons move and look like real minnows to the trout."

That line cut into my tender flesh like a knife. My visions of catching that huge trout were soon dissipated in the pain where the red mark of the line wrapped around my small hand as I obediently lifted and lowered the weights, made even heavier by the drag of the water. It wasn't long before I happily offered to return to rowing the boat and let Dad fish with the Seth Green rig. Dad just moved back into the fishing position like it was a normal transfer of tasks. He must have had thick callouses built up on his hands, because it never seemed to bother him. I can't describe how wonderful those wooden oar handles felt in my hands after that. The next time I fished, it was with a pole and reel.

Brenda Guidone

A Visitor In Jerusalem
Singer Bardin

It took me almost four months to reach Keuka Lake after The End.
It used to be a quick, four-hour drive from the city, but things changed
rapidly. The highways leading out of the city were clogged with cars.
The bridges started to fall apart almost immediately. Once I cleared
the metropolitan area, the countryside was no better. It's amazing how
quickly nature swept in and took over. It was almost as if it had been
waiting all along to reclaim the world back from the presence of man.

I had spent the past nine years living in a small alcove off of one
of the city's old subway stations. It wasn't much, but it suited me, kept
me sheltered, and there were plenty of rats to eat, so I never got very
hungry. I knew something was wrong. I could feel it building inside me

20

for months before I decided to leave. I didn't want to die in New York City. I missed nature—so I raided a few supermarkets of rusted cans, packed a duffel bag, and headed northwest without the slightest idea where I was headed.

And then I found it... or it found me.

According to the map I kept with me, I'd come up from a town that used to be called Hammondsport and was wandering along a two-lane road that ran up the western side of Keuka Lake when I saw it glazed in a single ray of sunlight. The old green sign announced that I was in the former township of Jerusalem. I smiled. It was like something out of a movie. I knew immediately that this was the place for me.

The little stone chapel sat nestled quietly on a granite bluff overlooking the silvery waters of the lake. It sat downhill from the road, and the little painted sign was illegible. It didn't matter what it used to be called; it was mine now. Since The End, everything was mine. It had been nine years since I'd seen another living person. Nine years... it felt like twenty.

I walked down the path toward the front door and let myself in. The hinges cried and gave a little resistance, but I managed to shove the heavy oak doors open, and a sigh of stale air exhaled into my face. The inside was smothered in darkness. The stained-glass windows were all boarded up, so the little chapel must have been abandoned before mankind went away.

I tossed my bag down on the floor and a family of squirrels living in the rafters scuttled away, deeper into the shadows.

"It's just me, little friends. No need to worry," I said, surprised at how strange my voice was starting to sound.

Since The End, wildlife had stopped being skittish, and in my long journey up from the city I had made friends with many wild creatures... and then I ate them.

The lump in my throat was burning, so I took a swig of water and wandered deeper into the church. The pews were coated in cobwebs. The altar was empty of furnishings. The choir pit was missing its chairs.

"This will be perfect," I said to the silence. I stretched and walked back outside as the last of the day's light dwindled away beneath the ochre dappled hills.

I collected fallen limbs and made a fire pit out of some heavy granite rocks right outside the door. Once that was going in a comfortable blaze, I wandered along the steep side of the chapel and pried loose one of the planks of plywood covering up the window. It came right off in my hand and crumbled away, splinters falling down the stark incline to the lake thirty feet below, leaving me facing a beautiful window depicting that Jesus guy offering water to a peasant. It was nice and would let in good light for the few remaining weeks before the winter actually took hold.

I put a can of pork and beans in the embers of the fire and sat down on the concrete steps and stared into the sunset and marveled at its beauty.

The sky changed colors by the minute. The birds called out to each other as they rushed away to bed. Two chipmunks scampered by and dove into a hollow stump. I knocked my can of beans free of the fire and sat them down beside me to cool as the first of the stars popped out, like flecks of glitter on a velvet sky.

I ate the beans as the shadows grew long. The lump in my throat made it hard to swallow—like having a wadded up sock wedged in my windpipe—but I ate until I was full, and then went inside and sealed the door against the moaning wind.

&

I'm only fifty-three years old, but I feel much older. When I first noticed something was wrong, I was living in my alcove under the 57th Street subway station. It started with a sore throat. I didn't panic at first, because it was winter then and a sore throat was pretty normal. I just went to a Duane Reade and helped myself to the medicine to make it easier—and it eventually went away.

It came back just after the New Year. It brought with it a cough that I couldn't shake, and all the over-the-counter medicine did nothing to relieve it. Then one morning as I was reading on the steps of the abandoned library on Fifth Avenue, I noticed I'd coughed up blood. I started worrying then, but what could I do? I went about my daily scavenger life and tried to ignore it, and eventually—it went away.

A few months later, in the spring, it came back, and with it came a strange knot under my skin right beside my Adam's apple. That's when I knew.

My father had died from cancer. Both my grandfathers had died from cancer. My mother had a mastectomy just a few weeks before The End, so cancer was in my blood from the beginning. Every day was like playing Russian roulette with time.

All the doctors are gone. All the facilities that could have possibly given me more time… are gone. There's no hope left, and it's inevitable that my end is coming soon.

The sore throat came back this past summer, and never went away. Every minute of every day it feels like I've swallowed molten lead. The burning never stops. The lump grows a little more each day—so rather than die like a rat in a hole in the ground, I left New York City behind me and ventured forth. I had very little power, but I could leave. The idea of dying in that city was worse than death itself. I ached for nature, I pined for fresh air—I couldn't give myself years left to live, but I could do this.

So, you see, it was a blessing that I came upon this little stone chapel before the first snowstorm of the winter set in.

I spread my filthy sleeping bag on the hardwood floor in the choir pit and slept deeper than I'd slept in years. I felt whole again.

With shelter like this … I may last through until the spring. Maybe not.

&

The morning came and I poured myself into making my little church a happy home. After nine years living in darkness and only scurrying out to pilfer things from stores nearby, it felt like I'd died and gone to Heaven to have the great sprawl of all nature's magnificence lying out in front of me.

I tore down all the plywood covering the windows, and it bathed the interior of the chapel in soft, diffused, multicolored light. It made my heart beat faster just to absorb the colors.

I took each of the pews outside and hammered them until they fell apart and turned into good burning wood for my winter stash.

I went into the pastor's office and found bolts of fabric that were covered in mites, but I arranged them into a soft pallet inside the choir pit and made myself a rather comfortable bed.

The interior of the chapel sat bald in front of me, so despite the gnawing inferno in my throat, I opened my arms wide and spun around in circles like a fool, washed in dappled light the color of apples and lemons.

I miss apples and lemons.

I miss a lot of things.

I miss my wife, Teresa, and our apartment on West 87th Street. I miss my parents, and I miss my childhood home in Leesburg, Virginia. I miss my cat, who disappeared along with all the people—which I've always though odd, because no other animals vanished when The End happened. Maybe Mittens just hated me all along and couldn't wait to get away, or maybe he went with Teresa where she and all the other people went. I can't really say.

But right then, at that moment, it felt good to just spin.

My second night buried in a nest of old fabric was divine. I was literally as warm as a bug in a rug, and it felt good to have the peace of mind to know that I had escaped the city and found the most idyllic spot to live out the rest of my days. Sometimes in life you just know. When I married Teresa, when I graduated college, when my first story was printed in *The New Yorker*—I just knew I was getting life right, and it felt good inside. That's how it felt to be waking up with the sun that first morning in my little chapel.

I stepped outside and the air bit me like the prick of a knife. Overnight a chill had set in and curdled the leaves with frost. I started my fire and went about busying myself collecting more wood, which I piled next to the door. I had many plans for the day.

I cleaned out the interior of the church so that it wasn't so dusty and aggravating to my sinuses. I found several sheets of slate hidden beneath thin layers of dirt outside, and I brought them in and lay them on the altar for my wintertime fire pit. I worked for nearly an hour trying to open one of the windows on the lake side of the sanctuary to allow some ventilation, and I finally got it open about two inches, which would have to suffice. I finished destroying the pews, and brought those planks inside. I squirreled around in the back of the pastor's office looking for more things I could use, but all I found was an old box of moldy hymnals, a pitiful old broom, another bolt of cloth, an empty notebook and a bunch of pens—which I am using to write this down. I know the end of my life is coming, but the writer in me doesn't want to leave without a record. Even if no one ever finds this and it truly is The End of mankind, it gives me something to do while my food is heating in the embers. Writing has always been a good distraction from my life.

As I sat on the porch steps, wrapped in my old jacket, I watched the dried leaves roll down the abandoned road, I watched the geese flying over the lake honking happily, I watched the glassy ripples on the surface of the silvery water, and I looked up at the gray sky. It felt good to be alive. I will miss this.

The two chipmunks darted out of their hollow stump and bounced happily under the edge of the church. They didn't care about winter. They didn't care about throat cancer. I long for that kind of freedom, but it's far, far too late for me now.

"Must be nice," I said to the wind.

I guess I was busy lugging wood and setting up shop and kept my body warm, because once the sun began to set on my second day, I felt the ominous chill lacing the wind. I spooned some more beans into my mouth, and sat on the steps. I watched the heavy, pendulous clouds churning from east to west over the lake. The wind in the treetops caused them to sway in hissing gusts.

Something was coming. It was coming fast.

I finished up my can and tossed it into the lake. Watching things tumble down the steep incline was fun for me. I needed all the fun I could get.

I wandered back indoors and inspected my hard day's work. The interior was pristine, immaculate, glowing with afternoon light despite the cloudy atmosphere outside. The stained-glass windows made my heart feel full again. I took one of the planks from a pew and wedged it between the handles of the doors. Even though I was the last human on earth, it still made me feel safer to barricade myself inside. I wasn't afraid of man… but I *was* afraid of bears.

I wallowed down into my nest and started a thick book I'd taken from the library. My only companion was the howling wind pressing up against the stone walls, the pop of the limbs of the trees around me and the steady drum of my heartbeat. I made it to the fourth chapter when my eyelids grew heavy. I closed the book, burrowed down deep into the layers of fabric, and drifted off to sleep, listening to the crackling of the trees dancing in the ever-increasing wind.

Have you ever heard a tree fall? It's frightening, and if you're close enough, there's also that dull thud-shake when it hits the ground.

Outside one of the largest maples dropped and went careening down the hill into the lake. The moan of the wind was too omnipresent for me to hear the splash, but the shake woke me from my peaceful rest. It was just after two o'clock in the morning, and the world was dead.

I preened my face into the crack I'd left in the window. The frigid air bit my nose and caused my eyes to tear up. Fat, weighty snowflakes wafted in and landed on my cheeks. I pulled with all my weight to try to close the window, but it was no use. The old wood frame was swollen. It was open forever now.

I turned on my flashlight and slapped it a few times to get it to work. The blue beam of light filled the interior of the church and I stood in the center of what used to be the sanctuary and listened to the violence of the storm. The glass warbled in its frames. The trees cried out for mercy, and there was only me to hear them.

I stared up into the shadowy eaves and tried to locate the squirrels, but they were hiding.

I wandered back to the open window and shivered. The temperature was plummeting, so I gathered the bolt of fabric left in the pastor's office and tried to wedge it into the crack, but the push of the wind had other plans.

My flashlight beam played wildly across the windows, and just as I was about to surrender one of my layers of fabric off my bed to wedge in the cracked window—I heard a sound that caused my heart to sputter.

Boom!

One single knock hit the double doors of the church—so firmly it was as if it had been rammed by a tree stump. The door trembled in its frame; a shower of snow fell through the cracks from the voracity of the weight behind the blow.

I stood still. My stomach lurched.

I couldn't breathe.

The swollen lump in my throat was choking me, but I didn't care—I kept my eyes fixed on the black shape of the doors and waited.

Then it came a second time, with more insistence.

Boom-Boom!

I turned off my flashlight and whispered, "Shit," to myself. Was it a bear, lured by my light hitting the windows from the outside and ravenous for a taste of me? Was it another person? Was it my imagination? Was it the wind? I wasn't able to ponder it clearly before the next round of knocks hit the door.

Boom-Boom-BoomboomBOOM!

I stepped slowly closer to the doors and called out, "Who's out there?"

There was no answer, so I took another couple steps and listened with every molecule left in my eardrums, but the only sound was the twisting wind and the silky patter of snow falling.

Then a voice called out from the other side of the heavy doors, "Let me in, you fool!"

My knees turned to butter. I saw stars floating in my vision. I was terrified and not sure why, because for the past few years all I'd dreamed about was finding another living human to spend my time with, and here was one demanding entrance to my final resting spot. I couldn't move. I couldn't think. I took a deep gulp and the lump in my throat sang out in agony.

"Who's… Who's there?"

"You know who it is. Open the door right now! Hurry up already!"

I stepped closer. The tone wasn't friendly—it was pushy and threatening, but I had to see. I just had to.

"Tell me your name," I said. Only silence answered me, so I took another step until I was just behind the wood plank I'd wedged through the handles of the door.

"Stop dawdling and open up!"

BOOM!

"Cut it out! I'm coming!"

My fingers tickled the empty air above the wood, unsure of my next move, and then the man's voice cried out again.

"It's cold out here! Open the door and let me in before I get mad and knock it down myself!"

I didn't know if the person out there would murder me, rob me, or what—but I had to open the door. I knew what it was like to be stranded in the snow, and the sound of another living voice gave me hope.

I lifted the beam and let it go clunking down onto the bald wooden floor. I threw open the door to the night.

But no one was there.

I stepped through the doorway. The cold took my breath away, and I realized I wasn't wearing a jacket. I hugged myself and turned on the flashlight and scanned the fresh, smooth, powdery snow, but it was virginal and undisturbed by footprints.

Despite the evidence, I called again to the night, "Hello? Is anyone out here?"

I held my breath, hoping I wasn't having auditory hallucinations, but no one answered. No one demanded entrance. I looked at the slick white path leading up to the road above, but there were no dents in the snow. There was no one in the darkness.

The two chipmunks scurried past, skating on the glazed snow.

"What are you guys doing out here in the middle of the…"

I heard a slight pop and turned around quickly, my flashlight beam piercing the night, and immediately it hit dozens of reflective red orbs floating off the ground.

I took a step back and scanned the woods surrounding the chapel.

A trio of deer stood just inside the line of trees, watching me. I yelped despite myself. I threw my light around and noticed it wasn't just deer—groundhogs, chipmunks, squirrels, a single black bear, skunks, a badger, and a platoon of small brown mice all stood still, staring up at me.

"Hello?"

My throat caught fire and sent me into a frenzy of coughing. I doubled over from the acrid burning that followed. I took a deep breath and stood up, sure the spectators would be gone.

None of the animals had flinched. They held their position and held me in their steely gaze. Deer hooves pawed the powdery snow. Mice twittered and twitched and rubbed their cheeks as they all stood statuesque and poised in the gentle snowfall. Watching me.

"Shoo! Go away," I commanded, and I threw my arms up over my head. "Get out of here!"

The beam of the flashlight hit the lowest limbs of the maple trees, and I saw hundreds of birds sitting staunch and fixed, their heads cocked, staring down at me.

I shivered.

I felt the most unsettling wave of fear shake me, and without saying another word, I rushed back inside the chapel, sealed the heavy oak doors, and wedged the plank of wood between the handles.

I stood in place for a moment, listening to see if the animals would approach, but there was no sound of footsteps. The only noise was the soft patter of snow and the cry of the wind, but I could feel their careful gaze coming through the door and washing over my frail, frozen body.

There were no more demanding knocks. There were no more insistent voices.

I turned my back to the door. My footsteps rang hollow as I crossed the sanctuary. I rooted down into my nest of fabric to try and stay warm and prepared myself for a long, lonely, last winter.

Teresa Tomion

Memory of Tubby
Bruce Westerdahl

I first met Larry Tubbs when the Bluff Point Mafia gathered each morning out in Jerusalem to drink coffee and to plan their next practical joke.

Tubby, as he was affectionately called by his many friends in Kinney's Corners and on the Bluff, never said a lot, but when he spoke, his comments often revealed a subtle sense of humor that could catch you off guard.

The first time I recognized this disarming trait in Tubby, I had just asked him if he were a member of the Bluff Point Mafia. "Well, I think I am," he answered. "But I don't remember filling out an application," he added with a straight face.

On another occasion, at morning coffee, I asked Tubby what his plans were for the day. "Well, I didn't do anything yesterday, and today I think I'll just pick up where I left off."

Another time, when the mist hung heavy on the vineyards out on the Bluff, Tubby commented, "The fog was so thick this morning, I couldn't open my back door."

Years ago, I borrowed a pamphlet from Tubby that describes "the grape cure," an old prescription for healing almost anything, including "gout, diseases of the skin," and, would you believe it, "plethora of the portal system." The treatment involved eating nothing but grapes—up to eight pounds a day—and drinking nothing but fresh grape juice for weeks, or even months.

I enjoyed Tubby because of his unique sense of humor. I also admired him, because I can't remember when I ever heard him speak ill of another person. Now there's a character trait we could all emulate!

When Tubby developed a physical problem that required his presence at the Geneva Hospital three times each week, a long list of friends and neighbors volunteered to drive him there each week.

Obviously, there were a lot of people who liked and admired Tubby, and rightly so.

I never discussed religion with Tubby, but I do remember an incident over morning coffee at the Merry-Go-Round Restaurant that suggested he was confident about his future.

An atheist who was present had just been informed that when he passed on "he would be all dressed up with no place to go," and Larry laughed louder and harder than anyone else present.

We cannot enjoy living until we have settled the issue of death. I believe Larry Tubbs settled that issue in his mind and with his creator, and I believe that he walks with the Lord today in that special place we call paradise.

Sandy Shriver

The Googla
(Keuka Quartet: Part II)
R.W. Webb

Nora erupted out of bed, shrieking and drenched in sweat. The warm breeze wafted through the open window and did nothing to cool the house. It was summer. The wind was as heavy and as thick as soup.

Tom, her grandfather, burst through the door and lifted her up against his chest. "Nora, Nora... What's wrong, honey? You have another bad nightmare?"

The six year old couldn't speak. She nodded and whimpered against his bony chest. He stood in the center of the room, gently rocking her back and forth. "It was just a dream. See? You're safe and sound, here with Pop-Pop and Nanny. Everything is fine."

Nora pulled her face away and looked at her bedroom skeptically. The curtains danced on the breeze. The night was silent around them. She sniffled and, in a meek, mousy voice, asked for the thousandth time, "When will Mommy be here? I miss Mommy."

Tom sighed. "She's getting out of the hospital in the morning. I'm supposed to pick her up from the train station at noon."

"Tomorrow? Mommy will be here? Really?"

"Yes, baby—you'll get to see your mommy. We'll cook a big supper and eat dinner in the yard as a celebration. How's that sound?"

Nora smiled and Tom felt her tiny, ropy muscles relax. He gently lowered her back into her bed. The oscillating fan blew the viscous air around the room like stirring soup. "Now you go on back to sleep and dream pretty dreams. Tomorrow is going to be a big day for all of us."

"Okay, Pop-Pop. I'll try," the little girl said as she curled into a ball and clutched her favorite bear against her chest.

"No more bad dreams, okay?"

Nora nodded, already drifting back to unconsciousness.

Tom stood and watched his granddaughter protectively and then tiptoed out into the hall, pulling the door closed behind him.

She lay quietly with her eyes pressed closed until she heard her grandfather close his bedroom door and then she whispered as soft as vanilla, "Are you still there?"

The voice wafted gently through the open window.

I'm here. I'm always here. I'm sorry you had a bad dream, Nora.

"Mister? Can you keep me safe in my dreams, too?"

I can try. All any of us can do is try.

The little girl squirmed with happiness. Since her mother had gone away to rehab, she'd felt totally isolated. The voice gave her companionship and comfort. She smiled in the darkness.

"I wish I could play with you, Mister. You seem awfully nice."

Tomorrow we can play. Tomorrow will be a good day.

"Really?"

Yes, Nora. Pop-Pop is going to Rochester to pick up your Mommy. Nanny will be taking a nap in her chair like she always does. You can come to me then, and we'll have such a good, good time.

"How will I find you? I don't know where to go."

You know the woods behind the house?

"Yes sir."

There is a small trail that the deer like to use. Follow that uphill all the way and then you will find me.

"You live up there? In the woods?"

I do. I will show you. We will have lots of fun together. You'll see. We'll be best friends. You'd like to be best friends, wouldn't you?

"Yes, Mister. I'd like that an awful lot."

Me too. I'd like to have a friend. It gets lonely in the woods.

Nora squirmed under her bedclothes. "Okay, Mister. I'm getting sleepy again."

Get some rest, precious one. And don't you worry... I'll make sure no more bad dreams come to you this night.

The sapphire fog of sleep descended down over the little girl and she drifted away beneath a thin sheet and the rolling hiss of the fan.

The voice listened to the sound of her breathing and counted the stars.

&

Shortly before noon, her grandfather left to drive the two hours to Rochester to pick up her mother, Abby. Tupper, her grandmother, settled into her recliner and drifted off to sleep in front of the television like she did most days. Nora quietly occupied herself in her bedroom with a coloring book until the voice came to her.

It's time, Nora. Come play.

She whispered to the open window, where the voice always seemed to originate, "Is Nanny a-sleeping?"

Yes. She's a-sleeping. Follow the trail and let's have a tea party together. I have lots of chips and candy.

"I don't wanna get in trouble. You sure it's okay? Pop-Pop told me never to leave the yard."

It will be fine, Nora. Just fine. I wouldn't lie to you.

The little girl picked up her favorite doll, Miss Priss, and silently crept out of the bedroom.

She slid into her sandals, crept down the creaking stairs, and pushed open the screen door. She closed it gently, making sure not to make a sound. As soon as she was out back, she took off running toward the steep uphill slope that rose from the back of the property.

Good girl. Good. Run!

"I can't wait to have a friend," Nora whispered to the trees, clutching Miss Priss against her chest.

You can leave your doll. She might get homesick if you bring her along, and I would hate for Miss Priss to get her pretty dress all dirty. We don't want that.

There was a momentary lull. Nora placed Miss Priss on the ground next to a maple tree and pressed onward.

You're a smart girl, Nora. A pretty girl.

The deer path was visible between bunches of honeysuckle and wild grape vines. Nora turned and glanced behind her one final time and then plunged into the cool, shadowy forest with a trusting smile on her cherubic face.

"Youse can't be drinking and staying out late, no more. You understand that, don'tcha?"

"Yes, Daddy. I stopped drinking and doing drugs. I just want to be home, get my life on track, and help you with Mom. Why can't you believe me when I say that I'm done with all that stuff?"

Tom ignored her—he knew better.

"I can't have any trouble. Your mother is too sick. I'm doing the best I can."

"I know, Daddy. I know."

"Nora is a sweet girl. You've got a second chance to bring her up right back here at home, where you won't be tempted with any of those same *issues* you had before."

"I'm glad to come home. I was wrong to ever leave. Percy ruined my life."

"Percy… bah! You need to think about your daughter, Abigail. I've worked hard to keep her chin up over these past few months. Don't you go showing up, ruining what I've done. She's looking forward to you coming home."

"I'm looking forward to being back with her, too. She's what kept me going while I was getting clean. I screwed up and now I have a chance to fix it. Trust me, Dad—you don't have to keep lecturing me. I'm going to make you proud."

Tom screwed his face up with skepticism.

"I hope your Mom is able to keep an eye on her today. She's been feeling awfully weak. The chemo is wearing her out, God bless her soul."

"Here comes the exit, Daddy. Look, that old run-down diner is still standing! I can't believe that. Nothing has changed. Feels like I never left."

"Good. Remember that. Maybe this will be the best thing to ever happen to you," Tom said as he veered off the interstate toward the small, two-lane strip of asphalt that would lead them up the valley toward Hammondsport.

The pickup truck pulled into the driveway, crunching gravel under its bald tires. Abby leaped out of the cab before Tom had put the vehicle in park. Rushing to the back door with a smile on her face, she called, "Nora! Nora, I'm home!"

Her mother, weakened and weary from her lengthy battle with cancer, pushed herself out of her recliner with a smile on her face. She hugged Abby as tightly as she could, but the young woman was eager to see her daughter.

"She's upstairs in her room playing," Tupper said, and then plopped back down into the recliner, exhausted from standing. She heaved a sigh and wiped her forehead with a damp paper towel.

Abby sprung up the stairs and searched all the rooms—but there was no Nora. She came back down, disheveled and sweaty, just as Tom was entering through the back door.

"She's not up there."

Tom frowned. "She's gotta be around here somewhere. She never wanders." He turned and walked back outside, calling his granddaughter with a booming voice that carried over the hills.

Abby joined him as they circumnavigated the small house, but there was no answer, and there was no Nora.

Then Tom spotted Miss Priss lying on her side on the ground. He picked up the doll and called Abby over.

"Her doll was lying over there by that bush. You don't suppose she's playing up the hill, do you? That's no place for a six-year-old."

"How would I know, Daddy? You guys were supposed to be

watching her!"

He stared uphill at the burgeoning forest that rose steeply from their yard. He stepped toward the small gash in the vegetation that deer and fox used and called a few more times, but there was no answer.

Tupper appeared through the dirty screen in the back door and asked, "What's wrong? Where's Nora?"

Tom didn't answer. He marched through the door and picked up the phone and rang the police.

&

"It's so quiet here," Nora whispered, even though she was leagues from anyone who could hear her. She spoke softly into the mouth of a cave, hidden by tendrils of vines and green wooly moss.

That's why I like it here. I like the silence. For many years, the silence has been my only friend. Now I have you.

The little girl turned and looked down into the valley. The view from the cliff was amazing. "Can you come out here so's I can see you, Mister?"

No, dear. I can't. The sunlight burns my eyes.

"How will we play?"

We can play later, once the sun goes behind the hills and the night bird sings its song to the moon. Then I can come out. Then you can see me.

"Can we play games like in school?"

Of course we can. We can do anything… together.

"That's swell, Mister. I've been awfully lonesome since Mommy went into the hospital. Nanny and Pop-Pop are nice and all… but it's not the same as having a good friend like you."

That's a sweet girl.

"What's your name, Mister?"

I don't have a name. I am nameless.

"Everyone has a name."

Some people call me The Googla, but you can keep calling me Mister, if you want to. I like it. It sounds better.

"The Googla? That's a silly name." Nora looked around at the forest squeezing in around them and asked, "Hey, Mister, where do you take baths?"

I bathe in the lake. The lake gives me life.

"I don't understand. The lake isn't for bathing, silly—it's for fishing and swimming."

I do that, too.

Nora turned back to the cave entrance and asked, "How long have you lived here? In the cave, I mean…"

At first Mister didn't respond. The wind crackled the leaves on the trees and clouds swept heavily past the honey-colored sun. Then, just as a blue jay was calling from a nearby branch, Mister's soothing voice oozed out of the cave, as soft as melted butter.

I've lived here forever. Long before people came to this valley. Long before the mountains were covered with trees. I've lived here a very, very long time, my Nora.

Nora scratched her chin thoughtfully and replied, "You must be terribly old."

Yes. Terribly.

The overzealous, small-town police department sent every officer on duty, and they filled the small kitchen. Tom tried to calmly explain the possible places Nora would have gone, showing the officers Miss Priss and steadily pointing toward the gash between the honeysuckle and grape vines at the foot of his property. Tupper wept quietly in her recliner. Abby paced and smoked in the backyard.

"This is some kind of test," Abby mumbled to herself. "After all I've gone through to get clean… this is some kind of test."

The officers placated the old man and disbanded out into the back yard, where Abby angrily marched out of their sight, around the front of the house. Chain-smoking was all she could do to take the edge off anymore. She didn't want to answer questions. She didn't want prying, judgmental eyes scanning her, since everyone in town knew her story. She wanted to disappear. She wanted Nora, she wanted her life back. But as the uniformed policemen organized a search party in the back yard, Abby snuffed out another cigarette in the front yard… and then remembered the shed.

She walked around the opposite side of the house, ducked inside the small cool shed, and closed the door behind her. She moved a few damp cardboard boxes out of the way and found Tom's stash of whiskey hidden on a small shelf out of Tupper's prying view.

There was a moment of hesitation as she held the bottle in front of her. She listened through the plywood door as the radios crackled and another vehicle turned into her parents' drive, and then she unscrewed the lid and took three deep belts of the warm liquor. The heat bled through her, and within seconds she felt like her stronger self again, without a trace of remorse.

She took another deep drag from the neck of the bottle and closed her eyes, relishing in the feeling of alcohol entering her blood stream after the agonizing months of sobriety.

She hid the bottle back in its shadowy spot and threw the door of the shed open. The sunlight suddenly seemed ten times brighter as she bellowed to the meandering cops, "Don't just stand there with your thumbs up your asses! Go find my daughter you lazy, good-for-nothing hicks!"

The news of the missing six-year old spread through Hammondsport like fog off the lake. Within an hour, most of the town had turned out to pitch in with the search. Hunters, farmers, housewives, children, church members, grocery boys, truck drivers, postal workers, crossing guards—all parked along the street leading up to Tom and Tupper's home. They all dove eagerly into the search for the missing child.

The mountain behind Tom and Tupper's house wasn't much of a mountain, but more of a glorified hill—as were most of the mountains cradling Keuka Lake. To all involved, the search would be a quick and easy undertaking. She couldn't have gone that far.

With eyes on an easy victory, the people of Hammondsport scattered up the slope behind the house and vanished into the trees like a swarm of insects. The police captain and Abby stayed on the small trail that wound its way around the edges of the slope, but the rest of the participants formed a combing line that went straight up the side of the hill. There was a sense of excitement, like at a church picnic or a festival. No one seemed worried. They were all simply seeking a mischievous child who'd wandered too far.

It was shortly past five o'clock and the sunlight had turned the sky violet. The clouds sweeping over the lake were rose colored and gilded on the edges by the setting sun.

Night was coming, but everyone involved in the search for Nora was optimistic that this would all be over within the hour.

It would not.

They are searching for you. They are looking in the wrong place.
"Oh no."

Grown-ups can be so silly sometimes, don't you think?

"I should go. I don't wanna get in trouble, Mister."

You won't, my darling.

"Is Mommy with them? Is Mommy okay?"

Everything is fine, dearest one… and night is approaching. Night, when we can play.

"I wanna go home. I wanna see my Mommy."

You can't go yet. We haven't had a chance to play.

"Well… I'm hungry, Mister. Do you have any tater chips or anything in there I could eat while I wait out here? I'm awful bored and awful hungry."

There was a brief rustling sound from inside the yawning cave, and then a bag of potato chips slid out from the darkness along the bald, black earth. Nora snatched them open and devoured them with relish.

"Thank you, Mister. These are my favorites. Pop-Pop gets these for me every time he goes to the grocery store."

I know they're your favorites. That's why I got them.

"You're smart, Mister."

I know everything about you, Nora, my sweet little berry. Now, we must stop talking for a bit. We must be as quiet as tiny baby mice.

"Okay," Nora whispered, and stuffed a handful of chips into her mouth.

The people reached the summit of the mountain and drizzled down the back side. Cluster by cluster, people gave up and returned home as the sun dipped behind the far hills and turned the sky lavender.

Abby felt disheartened when the captain told her that since the entire mountain had been combed, it was best for them to all go home and wait for news. The police would continue looking through the night, and in the morning they would call in the county patrol unit, get a helicopter, some dogs, and begin a more aggressive investigation of the surrounding hills. Abby ground the last cigarette in her pack firmly under her heel and, with a stiff jaw, turned and marched downhill toward her parent's house—furious at the inability of all the townsfolk to find one missing child.

Bad thoughts began racing through her head as she walked home. Tom and Tupper were sitting at the outside picnic table waiting for her as she appeared through the bushes, the captain bringing up her heels with a face lined with disappointment. Abby shook her head to indicate there was no news and stormed into the house, marched upstairs, and drew herself a bath. She was covered in ticks.

The captain exchanged a few hopeful words with Tom, and then regrouped his forces at the bottom of the driveway as they prepared for another, more copious, nighttime search of the area.

Tom helped Tupper off the bench and escorted his worried wife inside before the mosquitos came out to play.

Night was coming… and coming fast.

An hour after sunset, an Amber Alert was issued, and signs along I-86, I-390, Route 54 and Route 14A were all lit up with information about Nora.

With each passing minute, Abby became more besieged with grief over her missing daughter. Tom put his wife to bed after feeding her broth for dinner and did his best to console his daughter, but nothing seemed to help. Abby was sullen, angry, bitter, and fueled with animosity toward both her parents for allowing this to happen.

Tom sat with her on the porch swing while she smoked until the uncomfortable silence and her lack of engaging in comforting small talk drove him back indoors to the safety of the television.

As soon as she was alone, Abby crept down the front porch steps and returned to the bottle in the shed.

With every new drink she took, she became more frustrated and belligerent toward her parents and their inability to monitor a tiny six-year-old. As fantasies of the horrors Nora must be facing became more and more dramatic in her imagination, she felt the need to drown the thoughts away in the sweet, smoky liquid that filled her body with strength. So she did.

She sat on the small wooden ramp that led up to the shed door and watched as Tom turned the lights out in the kitchen, the living room, and then the back yard. He stepped into the doorway and found her in the golden light spilling in a rectangle across the yard. She was a hazy shadow, saturated in the alcohol she'd sworn to never taste again, but he couldn't make out the fine details of his daughter's relapse. All Tom could see was a shape in the darkness—shades of black on black.

Tom cupped his hands around his mouth and called out, "Abby, honey—I'm going upstairs to bed. It's been a long day. Wake me if you hear anything, okay?"

She waved and said something that resembled, "I will. Good night, Dad."

Tom stepped into the house and disappeared from view.

Abby sat on the ramp and finished off the bottle of liquor as the night aged around her.

The piercing eye of the sun woke her at dawn. After being clean for months, the heavy drinking made her head feel like it was full of rocks. Throbbing, angry, swollen rocks.

She pushed herself off the ground, hid the empty bottle, and brushed the dirt from her jeans.

Rushing inside, she brushed her teeth and spritzed herself with perfume to cover the stale stench of the whiskey, and then hustled into the kitchen to fix a pot of coffee.

A moment later, the floorboards above her head creaked, and then slow, sleepy footsteps came plodding down the old staircase.

Her father looked older than he had the following day. She could tell time was marching slowly forward, and she had a mental fast-forward to the fact that both of her parents would be gone soon. She felt bad about falling off the wagon, but with her first sip of coffee, she re-swore off alcohol for good.

If you'll just return Nora to me safe and sound, I'll never touch the stuff again, she prayed to the God she didn't truly believe in as her father pulled himself up to the breakfast bar and poured himself a cup.

"You been up all night?" Tom asked. "I guess there's no news then, huh?" Abby shook her head and sat down across from him.

"No news is good news, I suppose," Tom stirred more sugar in his cup and took a sip.

The floorboards creaked again and they both listened as Tupper made her way down like a corpse returning from the grave. Abby cut her eyes to her father and saw the pain looming deep behind them. Cancer was stealing his wife. Cancer was ripping through their savings. Cancer was all either of them thought about anymore.

Tupper appeared at the bottom of the staircase looking more tired than she had the night before. Sleep did nothing to rejuvenate her. Every day was an endeavor in staying alive. She looked around without speaking and didn't see Nora. She shook her head and slowly lowered herself into her recliner without a sound.

"I suppose I should call over to the police department and see what the status is. Captain said if they didn't turn anything up over night, they'd be calling in the helicopters and dogs to help in the search today."

"Mmhmm." Abby took another sip and felt her heart sink in her chest.

Tom stepped into the living room and sat down on the sofa across from his wife. He picked up the phone and dialed the local police department. "This is Tom Templeton, grandfather of the missing girl. Can I speak with the captain, please?"

Abby finished her coffee, turned to put her cup in the sink, and shrieked in horror.

Nora stood framed in the doorway, her muddy dress torn, brambles tangled in her tangled hair. She widened her heavy eyes at the sudden sight of her mother... and smiled.

"Hi, Mommy! You're here!"

Abby sprung through the back door and lifted her little girl into the air. Tears of relief rained from her eyes.

"Oh, thank you God! Nora, baby—where have you been? We've been worried sick! We called the police and the whole town came out to look for you! Where have you been all night?"

The sleepy little child blushed beneath the layer of dried mud.

"I was with my friend, The Googla. We were playing and he let me spend the night on his bed made of leaves and fur 'cause it was so late. He called them pelts but I don't think that's a real word. I didn't mean to worry you, Mommy! Honest!"

Tom roared out of the back door like a bear, his face screwed up in anger... and relief. "You damned little fool! Where did you go? You had the whole town worried sick, you understand? That was a bad thing you did, running off like that! Answer me, young lady!"

"Dad, please..."

"I'm sorry Pop-Pop. I didn't mean to scare anyone. I was just playing and then I got tired and fell to sleep."

48

Abby looked at her father. His eyes glistened beneath their wooly brows. He pressed, "You didn't tell us where you were."

"She said she was playing… with her friend," Abby answered as Nora lowered her head to her mother's shoulder.

"What friend? Who?"

Drifting off to sleep, the little girl answered quietly, "He said he don't have a name like us, but some people call him The Googla. I call him Mister 'cause he likes it better. He's awfully nice and had lots of chips and candy."

"Oh… no," Abby said, imagining the most graphic molestation possible. "Did he hurt you, sweetheart? Did he touch you?"

"No, Mommy. He's awfully nice. We took walks, he taught me about birds, we held hands and sang songs. I taught him a lot of songs. He didn't know any."

"Who the hell is it, I'd like to know," Tom demanded.

"He's my friend and he lives in a cave. He's very, very old but he's super nice to me, Pop-Pop. Don't be mad. He made me a nice nest out of furs and when I got sleepy, he kept me warm by covering me with his tail."

"His… what?"

Abby shook the sleepy little girl. "Nora, wake up. Did you say he had a tail?"

Nora nodded, her tiny head lolling loose on her neck.

"Yes, Mommy. It's big and lumpy and green, but it's awfully warm. He's got big black eyes and long pointy fingers. He had lots of candy and snacks just for me, but he didn't eat any himself because he only likes to eat chipmunks and squirrels and sometimes fish. Don't be mad. Googla is nice. I won't go away again, though—it's a long way to walk and I got awful tired. He said next time he would come play with me here instead. I won't worry no one anymore, I'm real sorry, Pop-Pop.

Googla is my friend. Don't be," she yawned. "Don't be mad. Googla…
Mister is my best… friend. He loves me."

That's right, Nora. I do.

Nora smiled and put her thumb in her mouth; smiling at the voice
only she could hear.

"Big green tail? Black eyes? What the hell is she talking about?
None of that makes any sense," Tom snarled. "I'll have the police find
this Mr. Googla fella and bring him in on charges of kidnapping, see
if I don't! I'm not gonna stand for this. Not if this freak thinks he's
coming onto my property, messing with my granddaughter. Can you
show us where this cave is, Nora? Nora? NORA!"

Nora didn't answer; she was swept away to sleep in her
mother's arms.

"Daddy, stop yelling. She's asleep," Abby said, holding her
daughter tight against her chest. "It's probably some imaginary friend
she made up. We'll find out more when she wakes up. Just calm down.
Your blood pressure, remember?"

"Fine," Tom spat and opened the screen door. "But this isn't over.
I'm gonna get some answers."

The three of them walked into the house as a new day in
Hammondsport came to life.

Something rustled in the bushes, and then all was still and golden.

Mark Moniot

How Do You Live with a Ghost?
R. Murphy

Dear Alex—

After gazing out the window at my quiet lake and mulling over your question for a few minutes, I decided to ask Bob, the ghost who stops by pretty regularly, his thoughts on the topic. He'd drifted in early, which was unusual since we tend to chat at dinnertime. Between you, me, and the lamp-post, I don't know why I even bothered. Bob's rarely much help when it comes to practical matters, and he's even less useful early in the morning.

"So Alex wants to know, Bob, how I live with a ghost," I tossed out, my fingers hovering over the keyboard as I awaited his pearls of wisdom.

"How should I know how you live with a ghost?" Bob muttered, obviously in a bad mood. I suspected a little too much partying in his mysterious netherworld last night. "I'm on the other side of the equation here." He sat back in his chair at the kitchen table and rubbed his face with both hands, shielding his eyes from the bright sunshine flooding the room. That early morning light didn't do my rumpled ghost any favors, only serving to emphasize his oh-so-slightly thinning hair and the gentle cushion around his middle. His usually immaculate silk smoking jacket crumpled in all the wrong places. Maybe he'd slept in it?

"Look at the question from my point of view," Bob continued. "My assignment is to help a crabby, middle-aged…" Finally noticing the mutinous look on my face as I typed, he hesitated and back-pedaled. "Umm, I mean, my assignment is to help a put-upon woman-of-a-certain-age get a few things done. Since I'm the ghost in this scenario, I'm not sure I'm the right person to ask. I don't really worry about how you live with me."

Truer words were never spoken.

I sighed and took my fingers off the keyboard. Another one of our baffling conversations, circling endlessly around the drain before flushing. Bob and I had been at this for weeks—talking for hours at night to help me 'fix' a few issues with both my daily life and my non-existent love life. (A ghostly two-fer... lucky me…) Frankly, most days, the only issue I felt like fixing was the one in which I could show Bob the door.

Not that he's a bad ghost, exactly. As he diplomatically pointed out when we first met, he's not one of those young, thuggish spirits who throw furniture around and terrify people. Instead, Bob's ghostly toolbox consists of martinis, babbling, obscure references, and large doses of nagging. (For instance, his idea of great dinner conversation includes lecturing me on the menace of buttered toast. Or on the sex lives of newts. I mean, really... newts?) For a woman trying to survive the financial ravages of the Great Recession, I find that this 'haunting' situation, like most social media, sucks up a lot of time that could be better spent elsewhere.

"Let me rephrase the question, Bob." I tried again. "How could I, the hauntee, make this a more enjoyable experience for you, the hauntor?"

"Well, now that's a much better angle," Bob responded, sitting up straight and brightening. "You need more martinis around this place, for one thing. And you've got to do something about that awful music you're always playing, like that Goo-Goo Lady. Why can't we listen to something snappy once in a while, like Irving Berlin or George Gershwin?"

"Irving Berlin? That's the soundtrack that would make this haunting experience more rewarding on your end, huh? And more liquor? Don't you carry enough rye around in that flask in your pocket?" I shook my head in dismay. No way am I going to incorporate Bob's suggestions for improvement.

The conversation—as do most of our conversations—degenerated from there. When it comes to life with Bob, sometimes I feel like I've woken up in the middle of an Abbott and Costello routine, or a Marx Brothers skit. So thanks so much, Alex, for starting Bob and I down a path that provides a little more fodder for another lakeside squabble... oops, I mean, discussion. Sigh.

Cheers!

Roz

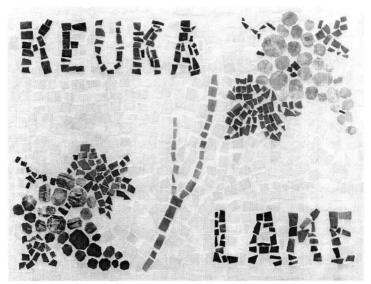

Jennie Snyder

The Keuka Lake Water Carnival
Collected by Debbie Koop

Every August during the 1950s to the early 1960s, Keuka Lake was the home of what was, in our minds, truly "The Greatest Show on Earth": the Keuka Lake Water Carnival. Preparations took all year, as people planned their performances and readied their boats. Morris Burke used his Cris Craft, and Bob Carpenter had his beautiful Fay

Bowen, named *The Spirit of Keuka*. There was a Century Coronado for barefoot skiing, performed flawlessly by a man from Cypress Gardens, Florida, and attempted and later accomplished by Johnnie Hsu, Bruce Cutler, and Rob Corcoran. There were pyramids and trick skiing and shoe skiing, and really expert slalom skiing. There was the man who put a chair on a disc and went by reading the paper. There were clowns and a dog on an aquaplane and lots of surprises. Rob Corcoran built a hoop that was set on fire, and he jumped through it on skis. Johnnie Hsu did trick jumping and 360-degree turns off the jump at Keuka College, and did flips on his shoe skis and skied backwards, too. Bruce Cutler, who built the jump, was the very best distance jumper, and also had funny acts, especially with the floating bathtub and someone taking a shower. Morris Burke always did a headstand while riding an aquaplane until his wife Selina told him he was too old. There were so many terrific and accomplished acts. Those of us who were too young or not good enough to be in the show dreamed of when we could, and we all practiced diligently to be accepted. Sadly, all good things come to an end, as did our beloved Keuka Lake Water Carnival. But the memories live on.

From Diane Carpenter Hayes: My memories of water skiing on Keuka Lake date back to 1956. I skied in the Water Carnival in 1957. Susie Lynn, a petite pre-teen, rode on my shoulders. She would hang on my back until I was up, and then she'd climb up on my shoulders. We were towed by my dad, Bob Carpenter, in his 26-foot Fay Bowen wooden boat named *The Spirit of Keuka*. I skied on my wooden skis, which I bought myself with babysitting money. From Penn Yan Marine, they were originally yellow, but I painted them black to match our Fay Bowen. I used those skis for 60 years.

From Laurie Petrie Heise: I was so impressed with the skill that Johnny Hsu had with turning around on his skis, salute the flag move, rope handle between his legs, going no-handed. I tried this, and tried and tried... and finally got it, too. I was so happy with myself to do a trick that Johnny did! I remember the skiers going up the ramp and jumping and flying though the air as they landed so steadily on the other side. I remember the girls sitting on the shoulders of the guys. They seemed so beautiful and strong, and the boys were so handsome. Oh, my foolish eyes! I was just so enamored with the whole event... the low and forceful hum of the Cris Craft wooden ski boats, which I can close my eyes and hear at this moment, the always warm and sunny days… the event of all events. Ah, the summers we had!

From Sue Petrie Locke: I remember Johnny Hsu successfully skiing barefoot. I remember thinking that we were all great slalom skiers until we saw the real "pros" like Johnny Hsu. That knocked us down a few pegs! We all wanted to try the ski jump, but our dad didn't approve of that activity for girls, as he thought the hard landing might interfere with our future reproductive capabilities!

From Ginny Wellinghoff Yost: I did an act on snow skis for the 1961 show. For the 1960 show, I was supposed to do a ballet act with two other girls. One girl fell on take off, which left her rope flailing around. Then the other girl fell and her rope was flailing around, and I was skiing all alone. So I had to make up my own act!

From Bruce Cutler: When I was about 15 or 16, I came across plans for building a water ski jump in a water ski magazine. I enlisted the help of an adult neighbor, Franklin "Hutch" Hutchings, to help me build it. He was an engineer with Bausch + Lomb in Rochester, and knew a lot about construction. He also owned a barn on the edge of the lake, which was an ideal location for construction. I collected some money from contemporary skiers in our area, and we built the jump in Hutch's barn. It was 10x25 feet. I was able to buy some used maple flooring from a scrap yard in Rochester, which we used to make the deck. We smoothed out the deck with a rented floor sander, followed by several coats of polyurethane. When we were done, it looked like a floating dance floor!

The jump was adjustable from three to six feet, so we were able to start low and work up to the standard jumping height of six feet. We had no instruction, so we made every mistake possible, but fortunately there were no serious injuries. We learned how to jump for distance, and to do a few tricks. At one point we had three skiers go over the jump at once (which was pretty crowded). We also had two skiers go over the jump while a third cut under the two in the air. Johnnie Hsu could do a 360-degree turnaround on the jump!

By the end of the second year, we learned that maple does not do well when continuously submerged. The leading edge of the jump began to rot. We pulled the jump out and replaced the deck with three-quarter-inch marine plywood. We were back to a beautiful surface that did much better in the water. We had a couple of good years using the jump, although it took up all our beach when we pulled it out in the winter.

Unfortunately, all the fun came to an end in 1960, when an intoxicated couple struck the ski jump at night with their outboard. Miraculously, no one was hurt, but my parents had had enough and we donated the jump to the Water Ski Club in Penn Yan. Because of its size, it took a full day to tow it from our cottage at the end of the Bluff to Penn Yan. The jump lasted another couple of years, then fell into disrepair.

The Water Carnivals were held at Red Jacket Park. They were only loosely organized. Interested skiers practiced on their own, but the whole show was put together on "game day"! We had a mimeographed program donated by Benson Photography on Elm Street.

We had a good variety of tricks, which included four or five girls on slalom skis holding flags; Ginny Wellinghoff Yost, Yolanda Wojak, and Rosalee Rapp were among the participants. Another act was a girl on an aquaplane with her dog. We had ski jumping, which at that early date was pretty unusual. We had a clown routine—someone in a clown suit, intentionally acting goofy on a pair of skis. I had Jeannie Wellinghoff ride on my shoulders for one of the early shows, which resulted in a picture in the *The Chronicle-Express*. Another time, Jerry Amann and I did a pass by the crowd barefoot skiing—we didn't make it all the way because of rough seas, but the crowd loved the crash landing!

I didn't ski the last two years (1960-1961), but I served as PA announcer. One of my best recollections was of the bathtub act. I think my accomplice was Steve Strong, but I could be wrong. We bought a bathtub from a scrap yard, together with some plumbing fixtures. We bolted the tub onto a piece of plywood or a barn door. We devised a scoop to catch the water and force it out through a shower head when towed through the water behind a boat, like a giant aquaplane. Steve rode in the tub, covered with bubble bath, with a brush to rub on his back. It was a very effective trick, and the crowd loved it. There was only one problem: the tub was so heavy that when the boat stopped moving, the tub quickly sank. So we had to start up and come to a stop in shallow water!

For the most part, it was a very amateur production, with lots of unexpected spills, broken tow ropes, and underpowered boats that couldn't get multiple skiers up. But the show was good fun, and gave us a lot of good memories.

Clifford LaBarr

Outlet
Alex Andrasik

The squall had passed, the clouds all blown into the east, and the world was pregnant with the after-effects of storm. The young man took the steps down along the bridge gingerly, careful not to slip on the slick treads. Heavy greenery from the slope on his left hung down across the stairway, and a brush of needles painted his shoulder with a wash of rainwater. The sun was warm on his face.

This was one of his favorite times, and he treasured it all the more for its lack of predictability. Some storms left the world in disarray and panting with exertion, while others traipsed through so quickly as to leave no mark at all, in neither mood nor matter. This gentle in-between suited his appreciation for proportionality: cause and effect ought to be perceptible, he thought, but he took solace in soft consequences. Anyway, the brief tempest had raised his spirits with its energy and beauty. More importantly, maybe, it hadn't blown his plans apart.

At the bottom of the smoothly-molded gray stair, he inched along the footing of the bridge above to skirt a large puddle of unpredictable depth that had formed across its base. Ahead of him, the swollen waters of the outlet stream churned against the grid of the little dam beneath the span, an echo of the storm just passed. To his right, the Outlet Trail passed through a tunnel beneath the bridge and curved out of sight in the lush, merrily bobbing foliage; on his left, it curved more openly, cutting between the grey-green waters and the slope down from Lake Street above. Light sparkled in intermittent pools, shapeless jewels on the paved track.

He took a moment to admire the rough stonework of the bridge, lifting his eyes to follow the span ahead as it passed over the outlet. It carried traffic and commerce above, blocked deadfalls and other debris below. Three years earlier, it had rained long and steady, and all the broken branches from surrounding woods had swept down the slopes and into the rills and streams, clogging many of them; the water had risen and flowed over the streets and into basements, and many homes and businesses were ruined. This dam was one stopgap, an important stent in the natural arteries over which human settlement had so long ago been laid here. Still, that spring, it hadn't been able to overcome the force and speed with which the water had rebelled.

The community had rallied, donations were raised, goods gathered, and the business of civilization carried on. There were still visible consequences here and there—empty houses, newly placed stonework that shone like scar tissue. He took a moment to marvel at the foresight of the village's earlier planners, and wondered what considerations were being made for the still-latent threats of future decades. Of course, he had spent most of that crisis time in his living room, watching coverage of local events piped through the TV station based an hour away in Rochester, so maybe his was not to judge the activity or inactivity of current civic leaders.

The young man turned left, starting along the trail as it led toward the stream's source at Keuka Lake. Ahead of him, a little spit of land veered from the shoulder of the shoreline and thrust into the outlet, carrying a ragged but solid remnant of an old railroad spur over the water. Across the flow, its former terminus still rose, or at least a part of it—a length of old buildings, once warehouses, perhaps, now repurposed into luxury apartments, a wine bar, outdoor seating. They looked crisp and clean from here, brown and white, convincing, but he knew that closer up, they were clad in plastic sheets of faux-brickwork. The railroad spur that once served them with industrial efficiency now ended only halfway to its former landing, access from the path cut off with a messy tangle of chain link. It was due for dismantling soon, he knew, to complete the effacement of the area's sweat-stained and sooty past.

It made for an agreeable present, and fit with the trend in small communities across the Finger Lakes, busily replacing their stalled industrial past with an increasingly tourist-friendly future, but the young man allowed himself a regretful sigh as he pictured the rail line's obliteration. He could wish for a little more cooperation between past and future, something like the High Line in New York, that brilliant repurposing of obsolete infrastructure. That was a railway, too, a line of elevated train tracks lofting above the streets of Manhattan's west side, snaking gently along second- or third-story buildings in Chelsea and the Meatpacking District. It had stood unused for decades, deteriorating and overgrown, the site of illicit activities both profane and sacred. But at least some locals saw its beauty and its usefulness, and some with ambition and connections had embarked on a brilliant campaign, and now it was a new park, long, languorous, sun-parched and bustling. Tufts of saw-grass waved at passersby, and carts vended artisanal ice cream sandwiches. Most of the activities that occurred there now, so far as the young man knew from his daytime visits, were entirely licit.

He chuckled softly, returning to this trail, this day. It was another former rail bed, with its own story and dreams of reclamation and development. So the locals were planning against future disasters after all, of the economic kind at least—as the rest of the traditional local industry continued to leach into the margins, it was smart to shore up its tourist appeal.

And yet this place, too, proved an attractive spot for an assignation, even as its 'improvement' got underway. His pocket buzzed.

where r u, the text read.

On my way, he replied.

He slipped the phone back into his pocket and continued along the path. This could be messy, he knew. Not just in the physical sense, no—they would be outside, that would help—but: inside. Personally. Dalt was nice, to the extent that he could know from their app-based conversations and their occasional fumblings in person. Sweet, funny (if overly given to text-speak)—and completely in the closet in this, his rural, conservative-leaning hometown. And as he walked toward this fourth meeting, the young man wasn't sure what he wanted from it. It was going on too long, and the messages had turned too personal to keep on like they were, meeting in the woods or in a car. He'd have to end it, probably. He couldn't do the closet, not at this point in his life.

It's not as though Penn Yan were an overly prejudiced place. Though he didn't go around announcing his orientation, he'd been open at work and with the friends he'd made around town. They'd seen him on dates, they'd seen his "safe space" stickers on his office windows. And he didn't get the impression, from the people he didn't personally know, that there was hatred seething just under the surface. Not much, at least. It was like a lot of small towns, though, where not a lot of people talked about things like that, where most folks wouldn't admit they knew anyone—the voice catches—gay, couldn't possibly have that in their family. No outward hate, just the little unconscious aggressions of people who hadn't had to confront a lot of that kind of different.

And Dalt was from out in the hinterlands, the wide spaces away from the lakefront and its cottages, from the main roads that brought the tourists—from the old rail line where, on surer days, clusters of people walked and mingled among the clusters of flowers, people from here and there, and where, decades ago, workmen and commerce and ideas had all flowed in together. Dalt's family was old, and traditional, and insular. So he kept quiet. It had never occurred to him to be anything but quiet, it seemed. Yet even so, he had started making hints, shyly mumbling as he did up his belt or pulled on his shirt, about something more than their quick trysts.

So this was messy. The young man wasn't sure Dalt would be right for him anyway, even under more favorable circumstances. Yet a connection was building there; he liked quizzing Dalt about his family history and local lore, and he liked the distant look in Dalt's eyes when he told the small-town boy about the time he'd spent living in the city. Yes. He'd have to cut things off before any more buildup.

All the same, everyone needed to blow off steam from time to time, Dalt no less than he. Maybe some boundaries could be established. A little personal infrastructure erected—a very proper emotional dam between them.

It felt good to be outside, breathing the storm-freshened air on the way to a little recreation. His apartment was stuffy with an accumulation of summer air that the fans and open windows couldn't beat back, and he'd left a sink full of dishes that had been staring him down balefully all week. He'd always been bad at just doing them, and once they'd stacked up, he'd end up doing them piecemeal across the week ahead. He'd do a couple plates and five or six pieces of cutlery, but just end up adding that night's cookpots to the mess, so he wouldn't really get ahead. He would really need to work on that, he decided. Later.

A couple came around the bend ahead of him, and he put on his nonthreatening-but-welcoming smile. They were middle aged, worn-looking, walking a curly-furred black dog on a red leash. They nodded to him, wearing their own pleasant smiles of hard-won happiness. The man was sleeveless; old, pale tattoos marked his upper arms, and wraparound sunglasses hid his eyes. Her waist was tiny, her face as finely wrinkled as the bar-stamped t-shirt she wore. The dog's tongue lolled, the picture of strutting canine contentment. They swept past, and the young man wondered if there was anything like that in his future. With Dalt? No, he couldn't see that.

He continued along the curve of the path, and the shift in perspective and an opening of foliage afforded him a sudden view of the alien new addition to the scenery. There, across the outlet, stood the rear of an old rough stonework building, a sharply peaked roof jutting up from its other side. But directly alongside it, out in the water itself, rose a wide, white, rubber enclosure, its taut, puffed walls resembling nothing so much as the world's most minimalist enclosed bounce-house. This, then, was the current reclamation project, the latest small attempt by a locals to clean up the poisonous messes of the past; whatever the stone building had been, it had not been healthy for this stretch of stream. Was this more evidence of laudable foresight, he wondered, or more a panicked attempt to mitigate an ongoing and all too present, if slow-motion, disaster?

Whatever its motivation, he was glad for the progress it represented, for the symbolic weight it lent to the notion of some shared responsibility, and a little care for the beauty of the earth. He wondered idly why it was so rare to see. Perhaps it was because progress sometimes looked a little too much like something Mulder and Scully ought to investigate.

He ambled on, conscious of the weight of the phone in his pocket, realizing his heart shied away from the prospect of another buzzing. To his left, away from the outlet, the ground sloped gently upward, then, as he continued, fell back behind a low concrete retaining wall, pitted with age. The slope was thickly overgrown with small trees and bushes, buffering the route of the trail from the noise of the road above. At one point, he came across a small stretch of the wall that had crumbled and left its broken rebar skeleton thrust forlornly in the air. Just visible through the brush, a drainage pipe protruded. Maybe it was its own discharge, in the rainy, flooded periods of the past, which had contributed to the dissolution of this particular piece of wall. Nature busy with its own reclamation work—a slower but doubtless surer prospect. He thought again of the images he had seen of streets thigh-deep in floodwater, of wrecked basements, precariously tipping power lines. He silently put his money on Mother Earth, quiet player of the long game.

A gravelly whir sounded behind him, intensifying with approach. Three Mennonite boys flew past him on bikes, one after another. They wore flannel shirts of the same pattern, and the same small round-brimmed hats, and fishing poles jutted from their formation at the same angle. An image in unison.

A little farther along, the wall receded entirely, and level grass verged the barrier of trees. Just a short way beyond the white dome, a narrow, lightning bolt-shaped trail veered up into the brush. Always intrigued by unexpected byways, the young man paused, peered up into the shadowed space. A little more delay from his meeting, a little indulgence in other modes of curiosity—Dalt couldn't begrudge him that, however impatient he was for company.

Up the little slope, shallowly positioned in the shadows of the thick overhanging canopy, a crude, low shelter had been erected. Its clapboard walls were roofed with stained tarps, tattered around the edges. But despite its ragged aspect, it seemed solid enough. Two bowls sat in front of its dark mouth. It reminded him a bit of his apartment, in some obscure way; the scattered leaves were like the junk mail he'd carry in and toss onto the breakfast nook, the draped makeshift roof like the careworn curtains he'd inherited from the previous tenant and hadn't bothered to change. But here, there was a sense of purpose, of old materials chosen and placed with care, recycled to fulfill a need.

The young man had heard of this: it was a refuge. Stray cats were profuse on the trail, for whatever reason—perhaps this had been a popular dumping ground for unwanted kittens, those who survived growing and interbreeding and establishing a fine colony of feral creatures. He knew that the local Humane Society practiced a regular catch-and-release spay and neuter program, and so the population had become more manageable as adolescent cats peeled off to find their own territory, or died, and fewer new litters were born to replace them. And here, in the middle of the popular walking path—or just off to its side, anyway—certain concerned animal-lovers had built this little shack, and kept it cozy with food and treats and water. And so it was a safe space, in its own manner—the young man smiled at the thought—for another brand of society's unwanted and undervalued. The cats were flea-bitten and tatter-eared and fierce, not fit for human companionship, and yet there were those who felt they should not have to suffer more than was their natural lot; that—as they formed a component of the community of the trail and of the lake and of the village—they, too, deserved a little care and consideration.

Two adolescent cats sat silently and motionless in the brush just upslope of the shelter.

He saw the glint in one's eyes first, to the left, and then, recognizing the texture and shade of its black fur against the green, noticed its companion a few feet to its right. The first was sitting in the manner of cats, upright and graceful and haughty, and a fern trembled from one unseen flick of its tail. The other was crouched, at its ease still, yet a manifest bundle of potential energy, its ears forward-pointed and wary, ready to move at a single wrong scent.

The young man froze as he took the two cats in—siblings, he supposed—then sank slowly into his own crouch.

He didn't think that they would approach, not really. These beasts were not for petting. Yet he wanted to take a few minutes to observe them, and he preferred to appear as unthreatening as possible as he did so.

They were a beautiful pair, green-eyed and sable-furred. Thin, he could tell from the jut of the shoulder blades on the crouching cat, yet not malnourished. They were neither patchy nor matted, but sleek, even with the clump of briars stuck to the sitting cat's foreleg. They each sat perfectly still; even the fern had ceased its tremor now. He could see that they both had notches in their left ears; they were "fixed," in the blunt idiom of mammal family planning—as if their natural state had been somehow broken; and yet, for the purposes of the community, they had been, imperfectly natural for the purposes of the trail.

They were beautiful, and they represented something—if not beautiful, at least sustainable. An instance of the infrastructure that governs relationships. And not just that—an altruistic infrastructure, one designed to limit suffering rather than to add to it. He stared at them, entranced by something within and beyond a pair of stray animals.

There was a skirling scratch on the pavement behind him. Another bike passing. The two cats' heads flicked as one, and then they melted into the green, a quickly stilled rustling the only mark of their disappearance.

They were gone, yet they would return to this place, when it was free of strange-scented onlookers and alarming noises.

He returned to the trail and stopped, one hand on a hip, the other shielding his eyes against a sudden break in the high clouds. He was thinking about the bridge and the dam behind; about what lay ahead, the playground he knew was just around the bend, the exercise installations that dotted the path; about the foot-beat trail farther along, the deeper brush, and Dalt waiting. He was thinking about the rough shelter hidden in the brush, about his apartment with its indifferent clutter.

As he started walking again, a little more slowly than he might usually en route to one of these meetings, he thought about the path itself, the Keuka Outlet Trail, and it occurred to him that what he was walking was a reverse stroll down the timeline of local infrastructure, bookended by the twin-faced and essential identity of the trail, that of transit: from tourist's walk back through the ages to the misty network of footpaths and game trails in a dark wood. From modern recreation he cast back, step by step, first into the industrial age, thinking of the ground beneath him with its history of wood and iron and steam, thinking of the stone bridge behind that had been necessary for the passage of trucks and wagons, and the dam to master the flow of water, and the long history of mills that ground grain and loaded it on train cars and into barges for transport up and down and away. And he cast farther back, into the subsistence age, seeing the frontiersmen in their furs, creeping along the banks of the water, knowing it was here that their quarry would pause and drink and rest.

Back he cast, along the receding trail of local infrastructure, through commerce and coursing and recreation, to arrive at simple pedestrian traffic, the movement from A to B, as basic as the walk from bedroom to kitchen for the first morning coffee, or from cradle to grave. All the external, formal infrastructure that he fixated on, he reflected, was built with selfish motives: get the goods to market faster. Build the bigger network. Minimize the threats from man and nature.

Yet in the midst of all the planned and the measured—the connection by design, and designed for the self—was that little piece of impromptu infrastructure, a coming together of people who may never even meet; they simply saw, individually, a selfless need, and then did something about it, together. They had built the shelter purely to make something better for beings outside of themselves, who could offer nothing in repayment, not even affection.

The young man was put in mind of an article he had recently read on the origins of the word idiot, which in the classical sense was not merely the lack of intelligence, but rather the unnatural disinterest in the public sphere; a turning inward that the Greeks found unnatural and self-destructive and, ultimately, deleterious to the public good.

He hadn't taken it so personally while the flood was happening. Now all he could think about were these cats, and their shelter, and himself—sitting in his unswept living room three years ago, a stack of dishes in the sink, while outside the water rose.

And here he was, on his way to Dalt and a little instant gratification, thinking about infrastructure. *Under structure*, in other words—that which holds up. That which is necessary for other things to be possible. That which uplifts, possibly.

He walked on, more pensive now. He barely registered the playground as he passed it, except to briefly envy the pair of teenagers drifting lazily on the swings.

He didn't know Dalt, not really, and Dalt didn't know him—and he was beginning to realize that it was by design. He recognized that he was holding part of himself away from connecting with Dalt: wires in suspense over deep waters. He couldn't shake the image of a bridge going nowhere, of a dam holding something back. Maybe this preoccupation with infrastructure came from his own abject inability to just manage the little things of life—the spaces around him and the relationships within them. He wasn't a dirty person, by any means, but he could be charitably accused of messiness; he seemed unable to overcome clutter. The stereotypical "neat gay" was a mystery to him, with his precisely arrayed bathroom drawers and perfectly squared-off artwork on the walls—a fastidious tribe to which he had certainly never belonged. Pens and pencils and endless pads of sticky notes had a tendency to overtake every flat surface of his apartment; his toothbrush and toenail clippers mingled promiscuously in a bath-room drawer, rocking in embarrassment whenever he pulled it open;

his scissors had no permanent home. The whole thing felt rather hopeless to him.

It's not that he aspired to be something that he was not. He just wished he could beat back the chaos—could demonstrate some counter to the manifest entropy of the world around him.

Infrastructure provided him a little comfort, whether in New York or on the Outlet Trail. To witness the ropes of cables and electrical wires that snaked into a port at the Lincoln Tunnel and emerged on the other end, linking and powering two sides of a rushing river, gave him a thrill of shared human ingenuity. But it did nothing to arrange the quiet tumults inside him. And he had done precious little himself to bring a little arrangement into the wider world, just for the sake of it. He was always following power lines and imagining how rooms fit together behind the regular anonymity of their walls. He'd spent half his life circling dormitory corridors and city blocks, waiting for a door to open, waiting for a light to change, waiting for a place to turn.

He'd never seriously tried to build a path through for something or someone else. He'd never tried to reclaim something old and run down to make into something beautiful—neither a disused railway nor a disused idea. And he'd neglected to consider that even dams have outlets.

He suddenly realized that he'd nearly reached his destination; he'd passed the playground, crossed the road, bypassed the tennis court and the forlorn skate park while lost in his reverie. Now he had entered a tunnel of trees, a wild space tucked away behind neighborhoods, and was about to cross a low footbridge. This was one of his favorite stretches of the Outlet Trail; he could feel alone here. Now, though, he just felt lonely. The shadows of leaves waved gently on the low span. He squared his shoulders and crossed. He was almost there.

Across the bridge and on into the wood, then, just short of another playground and a ballfield, still insulated from the lapping shore where the outlet poured from lake, he stopped again. A less-trafficked path turned off from the trail. It rose and fell in great humps of packed dirt, a rough roadway for ATVs. It was a quiet, secluded track that meandered back into the screening trees. He reached its end, a loop of dirt before a scrubby green curtain, and Dalt stood up from a half-buried stone where he'd been waiting, smiling tentatively.

The young man took Dalt in: tall, athletic, handsome, yet visibly wavering, nervous. He was another frightened being in need of a home, one twig-snap from bolting. He needed more than what they were offering each other. Walls or roads; dams or bridges. Something slid into place in the jumbled junk-drawer of the young man's brain; he felt the last of his anxious desire fade, yet none of his interest in being present. He didn't need to be the answer to Dalt's question, whatever it was, but he could let himself be one step on Dalt's path from here to there.

Filing cabinets, he thought, *I guess that's what does it. A label gun. Those little molded trays that fit inside drawers. That's what it takes. That'll be a start.*

But what he said was, "Hi," and stuck out his hand. "I figure it's time I finally introduced myself properly. My name is Adam."

John Tomion

A Winter's Lament
Alexander Wortham

The sun rose from over the hilltop on the backside of town—I always thought Hammondsport looked its best early in the morning, especially this time of year. Christmas is only two weeks away, and still here I am watching daybreak from my apartment over the liquor store on the square. I've been staying here since August, and I watched as the rushing summer crowds dwindled into an autumn trickle—that, too, slowly dried up, and now here I am, the ever-present watchman manning his post on the northwest corner.

The reason for which I had woken up so early had yet to be revealed to me, but I recalled a dream I was having that caused me to jolt awake. The faces and context were muddled, but I seemed to remember something of a better time. I rolled over and scraped the hair from my face and cracked the window and lit a cigarette. A few inches of snow had fallen over night, and the square looked frosted and peaceful—only a few cars were parked, and the majority of the businesses were closed for their winter hibernation. Not to be disturbed until the vernal awakening beckoned the tourists back, pockets lined with gold.

I hadn't planned on staying this late into the season, but after the grape harvest I just couldn't get myself to leave. There wasn't anything back downstate for me anymore, so here I am, leaning on an elbow with a greasy head of hair—blue smoke pouring out of the corners of my mouth like a tidal pool spilling its guts back into the sea. The apartment was warm; cozy, even, for a man of my current station, seasonally (verging on clinically) depressed, and technically unemployed. I could have made the choice to leave, but instead I stayed. I made a promise to myself last spring that I would come here and finish my manuscript once and for all. Things had been going well with my work, until my creativity hit a treacherous skid and I began taking long, melodramatic trips through my own gray matter, visiting places I didn't necessarily need to be. Lately, the nights had been getting longer and longer, and I was against a brick wall in my head. I hadn't been able to find a way over it, so I made the distinct choice to tunnel underneath.

By the time I got dressed and ready for the day, it was almost eight o'clock. I took a few sips of stale coffee and a bite of a sub sandwich that was in the fridge. It had started snowing again when I finally got outside, and with no particular place to go, I clomped my way across the square to get a newspaper from the Park Pharmacy—one of the businesses that had to stay open as a matter of life and death. Five months ago, this store would have been jammed with tourists buying their Keuka apparel and can cozies and bumper stickers. Now it was me and one pharmacist, woefully sorting pills, eyes gray and heavy, lab coat still as white as the snow outside.

73

With my newspaper folded tightly under my arm and both hands shoved inside the leather bomber jacket that my dear grandfather had given me long ago, I walked up the street toward the Park Inn. My steps were driven but calm, each one leaving a footprint behind me, and so far the only ones that had appeared. Not even Barney from the auto parts store had made it into the shop yet. Most summer days by this hour he'd be holding court on the front step, waving his hands in a flourish as he made his point at the end of one of his rants. Not today. Today the store windows were still dark as I walked by—the only sign of life was my own reflection.

The Park Inn was classically built, with large plate glass windows in the front, the name hand painted in gold for all to see. I always felt like I was stepping back into a bygone era walking through the doors, as if Glenn Curtiss himself would be there having oyster soup and a glass of Great Western sherry. The bar was dark and smelled like fryer oil and old beer; there was a large wooden sign on the wall that once hung above the Big M grocery store, back when it was called Smellie's Groceries and Dry Goods. The large beams in the ceiling and century-old burn marks and bottle rings dotting the bar surface gave it the kind of patina that was impossible to replicate. I could only imagine the amount of ruddy-faced boys like myself that had loped through that doorway over the years, looking for some answers or a place to hide. My own great-grandfather would frequent the place for gin highballs after his shift at the old Babcock Ladder Mill in the early 1900s.

As I approached the door, I saw one faint light glowing in the back. Since they weren't due to open for several hours, I knew Dell would be downstairs, embarking on his morning routine. He was an old man with an even older soul—the sort that one might equate to a grandfather or an old front-porch prophet. His given name was Ephraim Delacroix, but he just went by Dell. I saw movement inside, so I took a cold hand and buffed a circle in the frost so Dell could see it was me. They weren't officially open, but then again, neither was I, and it had been a couple days since I had seen the old timer. He opened the door for me as I blew a hot blast of air through my clenched hands and stomped the snow from my boots.

Dell put an arm around me and ushered me toward the bar. He shuffled his left leg and had a labored gait from a bout with polio as a child. His ritualistic morning sweeping had been going on well before I had moved to my perch across the square, but this time of year there really wasn't anything to sweep. He did it for the exercise, I suppose, or because he felt he needed to. Dell didn't own the bar; I wasn't sure if Dell owned anything at all, in fact. Summers he would spend his time walking the square in the afternoons, and by fall he would make it down to the water's edge by the old train depot. He never bothered anyone and never looked destitute—he was simply a fixture of this place.

I cracked my newspaper, and Dell poured me a coffee and set a saucer next to the cup, along with a book of matches. The smoking ban didn't officially take effect until the place opened, or so Dell would tell me. This particular morning I was feeling strange, like I hadn't fully woken up, or part of me was still fast asleep in bed, tangled up in the covers, waiting for the day to actually begin. I shook the feeling and chatted with Dell about the happenings in town, of which there weren't many. We both agreed that we had already had enough of the Christmas season, and we'd be happier when January hit.

Dell leaned the broom against the bar and reached over with a big bear paw and pulled the bottle of blackberry brandy out with a tinkling of glass. With a look at his watch, he poured two solid Dell-sized fingers in my coffee cup, before treating himself to some of the sacrament.

"What the hell are you doing here?" he asked, helping himself to one of my cigarettes. "You know, I was as young as you once, and I came to this town thinking I'd have it made—to live simply and to live free. If you're not careful, this town will chain you up. You'll be scraping change from your couch to buy a ninety-nine cent can of beer from the Quik Stop. Do you want that?"

"I'm sorry, aren't you the one that just poured me a cup of brandy at nine thirty in the morning? Unsolicited, I might add."

I wasn't in the mood to hear Dell's side of things, not this morning. I hadn't been able to write down a cogent thought in the past week, so I'd been deluding myself with draft beers and morning brandies to accompany my news and coffee. I would have given anything to spark again whatever force had been driving me all summer—pouring wine for tourists by day and churning out page after page of what I had heralded as quality fiction at night—all from my glorious roost above Weber and Sons' Liquor. I'd become frustrated with my current position in life just after harvest season ended. Second guessing had always been in my nature, but I was approaching thirty and without much to show for it. I began a destructive trip down the rabbit hole. Now it was the middle of December and my progress on the book had slowed to a glacial state. So for now I, too, would remain a town fixture. Just like my beloved Dell and the Park Inn.

By late morning, the once periwinkle- and fuchsia-streaked sunrise sky had devolved into a suffocating blanket of ashen gray. I abandoned Dell at the Inn so he could finish his process of opening—I assured him I would likely see him later, to which he replied not if he saw me first. I made the decision to walk back to my sanctuary atop Weber's, but this time would take a lap around the square before returning.

I stopped in front of the First Presbyterian Church and imagined my grandmother going to Sunday school there as a girl, ribbons in her hair and wool petticoat, her shoulders dusted in snow. The very same white steeple still towered above the tree-lined streets, offering a view that could only be shared with the birds. I wanted to go back in time and meet the Dell of that era and watch as he swept the ashes and peanut shells from that same floor—talking to people with the same problems.

The cold was beginning to get to me, so I hurried back upstairs—I thought I could at least bang out a few pages after my morning toddy with Dell. I had regrettably left my window open, so the temperature had dropped drastically inside—I lit another smoke and wrapped a woven blanket tightly around my shoulders and body. An old aunt of mine had knitted it for me years back ,and it finally made its way out of a storage box and was now a staple in my day to day. A mustard yellow piece as heavy as a lead blanket—it did the job.

For the life of me, I couldn't get myself to type anything of significance or weight, each sentence worse than the one preceding it, all of which stank like a ghastly failure. *What the hell are you doing here?* I asked myself. I promised myself at the end of the wine season, things would be better. I looked around the apartment and held my head in my hands, cigarette ash getting longer and longer until it fell into a mess on my thigh.

This was not how it was supposed to go. No, in my head there was epic cinema and romanticism surrounding the writing of this book. As I finished the final page, a glorious crescendo would take flight as I descended the stairs of Weber's on a bright spring morning. By then, each of the townsfolk with whom I had established poignant relationships throughout the winter would congratulate me and finally realize why I had been cooped up for the past few months. I wanted the lonely winter to get me there, one where I was the reclusive young writer living in town, bringing a tattered Moleskine to bars and restaurants, always scrawling notes and observations. *He must be a savant*, they would say as I twirled a piece of Twain-like hair and smoked cigarette after cigarette. In my fantasy, there was an end in sight.

So far, the only townspeople I had established relationships with were the bartenders and the locals who, I'm sure, at some point shared some kind of a fantasy as well. Maybe not all—there were some who worked hard for their money and lived for their nightly trips to Maloney's for draft beer and jukebox heroes. I remembered a time when I had the nerve to judge those people. Not anymore, not after my winter that had barely started, and not after my writer's block sickness had kicked in. Those guys down there could always turn a wrench and hammer nails, but not me. This good-for-nothing feeling had become persistent over the last couple of weeks, and until recently I hadn't been able to put a finger on it.

I decided that wallowing around in my apartment wasn't the most constructive thing to do, so I turned on the local public radio station, WQKA, to see what they were offering. While Bing Crosby serenaded me with "Silent Night" through my Salvation Army clock radio, I cleaned up a little bit, wet down my hair and ran a comb through it. I finished my sandwich and reheated a cup of coffee, and tried to pick myself up. The barren maple trees in the square and the salt-stained streets offered no solace to me, but I knew I had to make an effort, so I ventured back outside.

I took my usual route toward Maloney's Pub, where I knew I could sneak in for a drink before they opened, but instead I walked down Lake Street, toward the old railroad depot and the head of the lake. I imagined my grandmother again, pedaling her bike in high summer, dust from the roads stirring up around her while she laughed. The snow started falling again and crunched under my feet.

My mind was somewhere else now, back when I was young, walking to school on snowy mornings, wishing I was still home in bed. The apartment above old Weber's wasn't my home, though, and it felt like maybe it would never be. It was my prison that I locked myself in so I could live and feel depression and anxiety and loneliness all in one toxic cocktail. I thought stuffing myself away like a hunchback would bring me down to the level of peril I needed to be creative enough to finish my opus. And yet here I was, on a trajectory with an unknown flight pattern, from a point of origin that most would have happily accepted as *just fine*. So I walked through the snow globe toward the lake, trying to find some sort of relief in the quiet.

The southern end of the lake used to be home to mighty steamboats that would ship grapes and other goods from Hammondsport to the northern town of Penn Yan. From there, they would be taken down the canal into Seneca Lake, and on to the Erie Canal, and then on to all the major port cities. As I approached, my field of vision disappeared a hundred yards out on the water. The surrounding hillsides were shrouded in white, and a silence came crashing down upon me. Every ounce of me wanted to scream out and blame someone or something else for how I felt. *You were supposed to help me*, I wanted to say, *I was supposed to find strength here.* I didn't yell. I simply reached into my jacket pocket and lit another cigarette and watched the smoke disappear into sky. I thought of the old ship captains and all the people that had once bolstered the economy of this town then I thought of myself again. *Good-for-nothing*, I said.

I took a different route back toward the square, this time on Shethar Street, which was originally misspelled Sheether back when my grandmother was a kid—and just like that, there she was again, riding her bike down the street, weaving back and forth. I let out a reluctant smile as I reached the square.

It was going on one o'clock now, and a few cars had amassed in front of the Park Inn. I thought of old Dell and my assurance that I would be seeing him later, but part of me didn't think it was quite late enough. What if I ended up like Dell? Would that be such a bad thing? My self-loathing was catching up to me. Part of the initial allure of this town for me was that I wouldn't have any expectation of success or failure—I could just exist here as an anomaly, an outsider who was here to accomplish something that no one knew or cared about. I came here for solitude and surrender, but I knew I was also here because I was running from pressure and stress, and now I was feeling all of that at once.

I have a recurring dream where I'm sitting at a dimly lit bar on Christmas Eve. The kind where the neon lights cut slashes through the darkness and the motes of dust and cigarette smoke are suspended in each one. An AM radio plays scratchy, smoke-tinged Christmas songs from World War II. I'm sitting in the corner seat, shuffling around a pile of change as the bartender flicks his newspaper pages and checks his watch. No one comes in, it's just two of us and the darkness I carry with me. I tell myself I need to feel this way in order for the words to come so the pages can grow into a stack and then into my marvelous manuscript. I never thought about how I'd end up if the words never came.

I turn the corner and walk past the dentist office and the Village Tavern, and head toward my own light at the end of this day's tunnel. The porch of Maloney's Pub is in the perfect location—I have memories of sitting there on summer evenings, enjoying the tourists' banter with the locals. Summer time, Maloney's is usually a joyous place. I'd been there several times over the season, and found the mood to be quite light. As I approached on this snowy day, it seemed to be wearing a different cloak altogether. I wanted to hate it, or turn around and go back to my mustard-colored blanket and my poor, stubborn, untouched Smith Corona, but I couldn't. The neon signs in the window cut through the snow and clouds just like my dream, except now I realized that the lonely bar room in that dream was real life, and my corner seat was right here in town—a seat I set just for myself, pulled out from the table by some ever-gracious, ever-present maître d'.

I had to go in—not because I needed a drink, but because I needed to go deeper into this pit, to feel everything as purely as I could. The door creaked open, and a shot of warmth and bleach and stale beer filled my sinuses. And I wasn't surprised at all to find it wasn't hell or ghoulish or like entering Sodom and Gomorrah, but instead it was well lit, warm, and welcoming. Part of me wished all the other barflies were also there while I pined away for my words, so I didn't have to be the only down-and-outer in there. But alas, it was only me and Jacky Boy, the finest bar man in the area. He had kind eyes and a scraggly beard and a rotation of shirts featuring different taverns from across the Finger Lakes region. He had a pint on the bar before I could even sit down. I asked him if I could smoke in here, to which he replied absolutely not.

He asked me how things were going on the project. I told him slow and steady, which was always my reflexive answer. I didn't want to give away how I really felt about it all. It was my burden to carry, and even though it was classically the barkeep's job to offer guidance, I wasn't ready to lay it all on Jack this particular afternoon. It was only approaching two thirty, but it looked like it was already getting dark outside. The summer version of myself would have thought of this day and winced, darkness falling by mid-afternoon. But not this version—not the one who walked the cold square like a century standing guard, back and forth from bar to bar to apartment to bar. This version of me was perfectly dissatisfied with it.

I had a few obligatory pints with Jacky Boy as the daylight hours finally gave way to darkness. Around five o'clock, a few people trickled in, all of whom I had gotten to know over the course of my stay on the square. The first to come in was Harald; he wore the typical uniform of a winemaker in December: tattered Carhartt bibs, nicely worn-in logger boots, crumpled mesh-back ball cap. The dirt under his nails looked as natural on him as a tuxedo on James Bond. He wasn't too much older than me, and had travelled here from Austria as a notable authority on Riesling cultivation. He looked exhausted—a feeling that I'm sure he earned, unlike the feeling I was currently harboring. He sat and had a quiet pint next to me, occasionally fielding phone calls for urgent business up at the winery. A part of me envied Harald, tired and worn out he must have been, sure, but all of his expenditures were due to the pursuit of something he truly loved. I wasn't sure I could still say the same about myself. We sat and chatted a bit, which was always somewhat of a challenge, given Harald's heavy Austrian accent that got stronger with every pint. He was a good man—a very hard worker, someone who was clearly made for the wine industry, always joking that if he were to slice his hand on a sharpened vine, he would bleed the finest of Cabernets.

The bar room lights were dimmed and the noise was as muted as my senses had started to become. I counted and recounted my change on the bar and rubbed my still greasy, unwashed face with an open palm. I gave myself a heavy look in the mirror behind the bar, and somewhere between the reflection of my sunken eyes and the back of the Dewar's bottle, I knew I had to make a decision. I knew that in order to finish digging under my wall, I would have to eventually start tunneling up and out, instead of just down.

Yes, I came here to find solitude, but I also came here to find peace, and at some point along the way those waters were muddied. I lost sight of something. The eyes in that smoke-tinged bar mirror weren't the same eyes that were there months before—those eyes were resolute and hopeful and belonged to young man with aspirations. I came to the Finger Lakes for a reason, and fell in love with the people and the terroir in the process.

I thought of Dell across the square, at that moment serving gin and tonics to his meager bar crowd two weeks before Christmas, thinking that he may not even have a real Christmas. I thought of Harald, whose family was in Austria. What would they do for the holidays? I thought of myself, holed up above Weber's—or worse, my dream turns to reality and I end up in the back corner of Maloney's drinking eggnog, humming "Blue Christmas." What the hell is wrong with me?

I had Jack call an order in to Dell for a BLT to go. I once again trudged across the square—the snow had stopped and the night had gone crystal clear. The globe street lights and the towering church steeple winked at me as I passed. My hands were cold. It was the first time I noticed that the Chamber of Commerce had set up the nativity scene for Christmas in the Park, an event that brought all the locals together for eggnog and mulled wine. The Three Wise Men watched in judgement as I crossed for the fourth time that day. I retraced my steps into the Park Inn, where I found Dell reaching the punchline of a joke I had heard him tell fifty times before. I picked up my meal, and couldn't get myself to sit down for a drink. The Quik Draw screen was almost the only light in the bar, leaving an ambient glow of yellow and red splintering through the highball glasses, coming to rest in a pool at the far end of the floor. I picked up my food, left a crumpled five-dollar bill, gave a nod to Dell, and walked out.

This would be my last trip across the square for the day, so I walked down toward the water again, where it was dark enough to see the stars. The walk was clarifying and the crunchy snow kept a perfect rhythm, one that I was holistically lacking. I wasn't sure what I needed at this point in my life—I couldn't decide if it was to be able to finish my manuscript, or just find peace in the present. I found myself wishing my grandmother was walking with me, not as a little girl, but as the woman she was when she passed away, or the one I knew when I was a little boy. Was it wisdom I lacked? I couldn't help but think that I was missing something. I needed to tunnel out.

When I reached the railroad tracks again, the water was a sheet of glass. The sky was an expanse of black, and the stars were so thick it looked like a celestial hand had smeared a streak of whitewash from one horizon line to the other. I took a deep breath in and imagined myself happy and free—with a stack of pages in my hand and the buds breaking on the trees. I thought of Christmas and my family and the stool at the back of the bar and my grandmother and the choices I had made in the last year. My days had begun to blend together, and I could only blame myself, not Dell or the Park Inn or Jacky's perfectly poured pints. This town and this square cradled me and inspired me so much, and I had the nerve to use it as an excuse. My grandmother would be so disappointed. I picked up a stone and heaved it into the lake—it sent ring after ring outward until it flattened and the reflection of the stars regained control of the surface. I sighed and turned back toward the square. One thing was on my mind as the white steeple guided me back to my den above the liquor store: This town might save me yet—if I was only to let it.

Andrew Bell

A Great Ad-Bench-Er
Lisa Cavanaugh

There once was a bench. He was lucky, as benches go. He was
fastened to a dock and lived his days looking out over the waters of
Keuka Lake. He spent long hours propping up couples who enjoyed
happy, quiet moments together, people who read books as the sun set,
and friends who prepared for boat rides. He had been a diving board
for children, a drying rack for damp towels, and, sometimes—much to
his dismay—a litter box for the many seagulls that came to visit.

Overall, he was happy with his lot in life. Every spring, he was
content to sit and wait for his family to join him. He watched with
anticipation as the grapevines grew and the grass turned green. He
noted each forget-me-not turning its blue face to catch the weak
sunshine. He practically jumped for joy when his family finally

85

arrived, excited to start their summer adventures. He watched the spring cleaning, waiting patiently for his own yearly scrub-down. He said hello to Mr. Boat, who was put into the still-chilly waters, grumbling about it the whole time. He nodded at the tubes and toys as they were pulled out and left to sit on the dock next to him. He watched winter-white skin turn golden tan. He lovingly noted how much the children had grown over the winter. He was happy to host guests for warm evenings, soaking up the drops of good Finger Lakes Riesling that spilled on him.

Gradually, with sadness, he noted a slight chill in the evenings that turned to cold rain, and leaves that began to fall from the trees. He felt fewer treads upon the dock beneath him as the children returned to school and only visited on weekends. He watched his family pull Mr. Boat out of the water and winterize the cottage. He let out a sigh as they waved goodbye and headed back to their warmer home for the snow that was sure to arrive in the coming months.

The winters were always depressing for the bench. No one came to visit him except the ice, who spoke in an odd, echoing language. Some years, the ice and the bench grew to be close friends, the ice growing around the base of his dock, speaking to him in cracks and creaks. Other years, the ice stayed far away, shouting to him infrequently over the winter waves of the lake.

It was during one particularly icy winter that the bench had an idea. He was sick of the wind and snow. He was getting on in years, and wanted to become an indoor bench. The freezes and thaws were twisting his planks, and the sun's rays were turning him an ashy gray. He would go find his family. They undoubtedly would be pleased to see him, to caress his strong back and snuggle in on his broad seat. They would remark on what a wonderful and loyal bench he was. They would see his arching planks and realize that it was time to retire him to the screen porch. Maybe they would even give him a fresh sanding and a coat of stain.

"Hello ice!" the bench called out.

"Hello bench!" the ice groaned back. "How does this fine freezing day find you?"

"I have an idea," the bench said. "I wonder if you could grow this way, and perhaps help me to get off this dock?"

"Oh," moaned the ice, "planning on going for a swim?"

"No, not a swim, but an adventure! I want to go find my family. It has been so many long months since I have seen them, and I want them to know how much I miss them."

"Oh, going to see your family?" the ice responded. "I've never had a family, but I understand they are wonderful. I will help you on your adventure."

The bench was thrilled that the ice would help him. They worked out a plan: The ice would grow closer and closer each day, until he could pull the bench off his dock and into the water.

One morning, a few days later, everything was ready. The ice had been pushing and pulling at the dock, and the bench knew he was nearly ready. Finally, with a loud CRACK, his section of the dock broke free. The bench was thrilled! His adventure had begun.

As he bobbed along the unfrozen paths in the ice, he had a much different view than the one he had seen for so many years. He saw cottages, large and small, painted many different colors. He saw other docks, some bent and broken by the ice. He saw other benches, too.

"Hello, friends!" he shouted as he floated past them.

What an amazing adventure, thought the bench. *I'm seeing so many things I never realized existed.*

As he traveled along the shore, enjoying the new view, a thought suddenly occurred to him: he didn't know where his family was. He didn't even know how to find them. Most of the cottages were closed up for the winter. There was no one to even ask where to go.

Oh, no! thought the bench. *What have I gotten myself into? I need to go home!*

As he looked around for his cottage, the bench realized he had no idea where he was. Even worse, he was headed away from shore, toward the middle of the lake. The bench tried to shift his weight around and propel himself back toward his home, but it was no use. He was caught in the current.

The bench sighed. The piece of dock he was attached to was absorbing the cold water, and he was surely going to sink. It was only a matter of time before he ended up at the bottom of the lake.

For many days and nights, the bench bobbed along with his sad thoughts, his only company the slowly receding ice. The bench reminisced about his wonderful family. He thought of the children, now much older, who had played on him for years, and the adults who had relaxed in his warm embrace and taken such good care of him.

Why did I have to go on this adventure? thought the bench. *I had such a beautiful spot in the sunshine, and such a loving family. I am such a stupid bench to think I needed to find something better.*

The bench was so caught up in reminiscing that he didn't hear the rumbling sound of a boat, making its way carefully toward him in the gray water.

"Who do we have here?" burbled the boat. "You look like you're a bit far from home."

"Oh, hello there! I was hoping to go on an adventure to find my family, I've missed them so much. I am afraid that I didn't think this through. I have no idea where my family is, and I can't get back to my cottage," the bench babbled back. He was very happy to finally see someone else on the deserted lake.

"Well," said the boat, "I believe my owner knows where you live, and we're going to tow you home."

"Thank you, thank you!" shouted the bench.

The boat's owner tied a rope around one of the bench's boards, and started pulling him slowly home. The bench watched the lake go by as they floated along. He watched the cottages, big and little, and thought that none could compare to the perfection of his family's home. He also saw a few boats in the water, and lounge chairs out on docks.

Is it really nearly springtime? the bench thought to himself.

Then his family's cottage came in to view. There, on the shore, was his family! The boat pulled up close, and the bench could hear them calling.

"Thank you for finding our bench! He has been with us for so many years, we would miss him so much if he had gotten lost!"

The bench couldn't believe it. His family had missed him; they did think about him in the long winters while they were away!

His family pulled him to shore. They exclaimed how lucky he was to have gotten back home. They commented on how wonderful his strong back was, to have stayed together in the icy waters. They noticed that he needed a new coat of stain, and promised to do it first thing.

One of the children, the youngest daughter, said to her mother: "Mama, maybe we should put this bench on the screen porch next year. He has been with us since before I was born. I would hate to lose him if the ice came in again next year."

So it was decided. The bench would go inside the cottage after this summer.

Once his dock was mended and he was freshly stained, the bench was back out on the water for his final summer. He reveled in the warm breezes and the scents of barbeque. He enjoyed the splashes from the children, and the warm sunshine that dried him off. Then, as the chilly breezes of autumn set in, his family unscrewed his legs from the dock and gently carried him inside the cottage. The bench relished the new feeling of the indoor-outdoor carpet under his feet, and the wide view across the lake from his new spot.

As his family closed up the cottage and said their goodbyes, the bench thought to himself, *Adventures are wonderful, but the love of my family is the best feeling I could ever ask for.*

Judy Bailey

Cleaning House
Sarah Thompson

My husband died and left me the barn, the basement, the shop, the garage, and our bonus room overflowing with things. His writings I found later, after I hired the guy to come clean out the barn. *How do I know what to throw away?* he'd asked. I told him when in doubt, throw it out. We lived in the house 40 years. The wooden beams and inglenooks beside the fireplace shone after years of wear; when the sun came in the front windows, they emanated a warm, yellow glow, and we didn't need the fireplace on those fall days.

I have too much furniture for my new house. The heavy Stickley chairs and flower petal-shaped lamps don't work. I wanted to start over. I'm a tall woman. The old house was shorter than me; I bumped my head on the chandelier every night standing up from the dinner table. I loved that chandelier.

We never used the bonus room. Thomas was always either outside in the barn, his shop, or the office. Or with me in our bedroom. The first time we spent the night together I was 21 years old, in a camper borrowed from a friend. We talked about what we'd do after graduation. I touched a tiny rivulet of hair running down Thomas' temple. Travel, he said. Go anywhere. Together. He was as tall as me. We curled against each other and, when he'd fallen asleep, I dreamt of our child. He was golden, like the gleaming wood in our house on the farm in Pennsylvania.

I didn't know you could spend 40 years in a house and never know it. A young man came by the other day, before the moving van came, asking me if I knew a woman named Constance Egalitoire. I couldn't pronounce it. She used to live in our house. The man was short and compact. He wore heavy boots, a Carhartt jacket splotched with paint, and a beard. He introduced himself as Paul. Paul said he was the only surviving member of the Egalitoire family.

We sat in the kitchen and I found the one thing I hadn't packed: an electric tea kettle and two mugs. Habit.

"We used to come here as kids. Walking the trails. Sitting by the fire while Grandma played the banjo. Knitting. She had a wonderful voice."

I didn't know anyone in Pennsylvania who played banjo. It sounded like a Georgia thing. I was born and raised in central New York.

"How old was she when she died?" I asked.

"We don't know."

"What do you mean?"

"No one found her."

"What?"

Paul peeled off his jacket.

"I'm sorry." Paul rubbed his hand over his eyes, inhaling.

"I didn't mean to be spooky. But we never saw her again. One day she was here, and then no one could find her."

I placed my mug on the wooden trestle table, made by Thomas, on the same water ring I'd set it down on a million times over forty years.

"Jesus."

"I know."

I envisioned my Grandma Harriet, her sister Garnet, the other sister, Opal. A trio of white-clad ladies at a tea in the village of Pines Hill, around the corner from the train depot. The lake. There was a story they told us of a young woman who'd walked into the lake in the wee hours of the morning, during the first spring thaw. She found an expanding ice fisherman's hole and jumped in. Her heart stopped. Garnet said the woman had a newborn at home.

"I'm sorry to bother you, but I just wanted to look around once before you sold."

I felt sorry for Paul. He reminded me of Sam, my tangled old Cocker. I wanted to hug him. But I don't hug anymore.

"Sure, come with me. We'll walk through the woods."

We stood up, I whisked the mugs back to the kitchen, and Paul was out the door before I turned around.

The smell of Daisy and hay and wet wool and manure is Thomas' smell. Paul stood in the corner, near the rickety ladder that rose through the ceiling to the hay loft. When I stood there, like he was,

I sometimes wondered how rickety the ladder really was. Once, I stepped onto the bottom step, felt a slight give, and stepped away. It was too dangerous then, just days after Thomas died.

"We'd play on the hay bales up there."

He wasn't looking up there. He was looking at a spot near his toes. Then he was looking at me, cocked his head, smiled. His front tooth was chipped, a cap covered one on the bottom.

"Mrs. Dennis. This has been real nice. Thank you so much."

"But we haven't gone to the shed yet, the woods."

"It's okay. Already taken too much of your time. Thanks again."

He ducked out with a wave and picked his way to the fence he knew opened onto the road just beyond the gate.

My new house will be filled with modern furniture, all lines and curves. No more wood. I need stools for my kitchen bar. I'm thinking about metal.

When I was teaching tenth grade chemistry at the school, and Thomas was working at the factory in sales, I'd review my periodical table waiting for him to come home. I wondered why iridium was where it was. What was I missing? Mercury? Oxygen? I'd pulled my knees to my chest after every time we had sex. I'd bought the special douche bags and other paraphernalia my gynecologist has recommended, and then when he recommended a subscription to *Penthouse*, I drove to Village Drug and bought a copy. I drank a small thimble of Scotch; this was also recommended.

Those days, Thomas usually came home late with a bag of Chinese food. After dinner, we'd have another Scotch and I'd retire to the bedroom, find the negligee I'd bought at Dillard's once on a trip to the city, grab the *Penthouse*, and thumb through while Thomas washed up. I was amazed. I had no idea that women had this much power. The magazine seemed a testament to my Amazonian intensity, my ability to crush weaker men and women under the pointy heel of my thigh-high boots. Thomas thought it was funny. We'd throw the magazine on the floor and he'd remind me that most men would never attempt to get this close. Then he'd get up and I'd pull my knees to my chest, listening to piss splashing against the toilet bowl, praying for something to happen.

A few months later, I had my first miscarriage.

Paul left his address on the flap of an envelope on my counter. He told me to stay in touch. The movers came Friday, and I spent the day supervising. The house began to reek of sweat, stale cigarettes, and Big Whoppers. I shoved aside the several boxes I was taking with me and loaded them into my pickup, with the dog and my suitcases. I locked the house. It was dead too.

My new house is perfect. It's not on the lake, but I am familiar here, in my bones. The place you grow up is the place you are, no matter where you go. Tonight, I lit the gas fireplace and poured a jigger of Scotch. The fire set ablaze the white, white walls and red leather couch. I sat in the Stickley chair and opened the first box. Mothballs and mold wafted out.

The more rooms and buildings you have, the more shit you find to fill it. It was tough to get started after Thomas died. I would find something of his, hold it, smell it. Cry over it. I started tossing things into boxes: Keep, Donate, Trash. The Trash got bigger, the Keep got smaller. The first few shirts were the hardest. These were the trio of grays. Thomas wore a gray t-shirt nearly every day I knew him. These three were his most worn, the outer body he slipped over his inner life.

They had the shape and smell of him. They were riddled with holes around the neckline. But once I got over them—snipping the shirts into ribbons and burning them in a metal bin out back—it was addicting.

This box is a Keep. Box 1 of 3. First things I couldn't part with. A photo of Thomas riding the bucking bronco at a bar near the Pennsylvania-New York border. A plaque he was given for Salesman of the Year. A stack of letters he wrote his brother in Vietnam. The piece of paper I'm looking for is probably in Box 3. It's a birth certificate. And a death certificate. I'm trying to find David.

&

Dear Paul,

I am finally settled in Pine Hills and thought of you the other day. How are things? Have you met the people who moved into my house? Old house, I should say. You mentioned having no family in the area. You never said—are you married? I was thinking about your grandmother, and how horrible that must have been for your parents. Was it your maternal or fraternal grandmother? I know it doesn't matter, but I'm a curious person. I apologize for being so forward. This was something my mother always warned me about: Joanie, people don't need you poking around! Anyway, I hope you are well. I am glad to have Sam with me; it gets me out of the house. It can be quiet here.

Best,
Joan Dennis

&

Month One and I'm worried that maybe I threw something very important away. I tore apart the boxes and looked under the sofa, in the new basement, and in the back of my truck, and all that's there is dog hair. I cannot find the certificates. I haven't heard back from Paul, and am getting worried. Thomas used to tell me, the past is in the past, and the future has yet to come, so enjoy today. Bullshit. He would not have said that if he'd been the one who died first.

&

I was 27 and the tiny bean inside of me was growing. Thomas would lay next to me, placing a hand on his flat, hairy stomach and smiling.

"I'm jealous."

"Of my vomit and bad breath?"

"Of the amazing ability of your body to do that."

A month later and I could stand up without puking. I went back to teaching. I wore large, coat-like dresses to hide my bump. The principal was a sharp, wiry man who smelled like saddle soap. Mr. Hannelly called me into his office one Friday to discuss my "situation."

"It's come to my attention that..."

"Yes, Mr. Hannelly, I'm pregnant."

His eyes rested somewhere above my head, behind me. His hands clasped on the desk blotter, the class ring on his left hand digging into his finger. I watched a muscle in his cheek twitch.

"So, in light of this situation..."

"It's not a situation, Mr. Hannelly. I'm pregnant."

"Well, we should address this like any issue we'd address in school, rule-wise."

I was the only female teacher of math or science in the school. I was a unicorn. It was decided, per Mr. Hannelly, that I could work only until my "condition" became apparent. He was concerned about what teenage boys, not to mention girls, would do if they saw a pregnant woman up close. I reminded him from whence he came.

"That may be, but we have our rules, Mrs. Dennis."

Thank God I wasn't unmarried, like poor Amber Savage.

I went on leave after my fourth month. A young man took my place; Darryl Daniels never left.

Every day I walk Sam on the road and then down to the Outlet Trail. It's the bed of an old railroad, which is laid on top of an even older canal towpath. We crunch along on gravel. The water runs brown here when it rains, sweeping away fields, rocks, and sticks—clogging up to form makeshift islands, then eventually spitting everything back out into another lake, eight miles away.

Thomas and I hiked the gorges near Pine Hills every so often. When it was dry, you could walk over the limestone or sandstone rock beds, in the deep V of the gorge. The water had worn these places into symmetrical perfection, and at the end of this pilgrimage you entered a cathedral of light and water. One day a trickle, one day a waterfall.

Thomas once climbed to flat rock balanced hundreds of feet up, perched on a constantly shifting mountain of splintered shale. Touch it and a section would cascade down. It was a month before my due date, and we were still picking names.

Thomas clambered up as I looked, my neck thrown back.

"Be careful!"

He reached the top, spread out his arms, and yelled into the echoing chamber.

"I'm going to be a father!"

I held my breath until he was safely back on the ground.

&

There is nothing sacred about giving birth. It's like war, human and unstoppable. I was grading a paper for my friend Darryl (nice distraction and side job), when I felt a grabbing of my low abdomen, then a knife in my low back. I crumpled forward. Thomas was at work. It was early. Not so early, but early. I practiced the breathing. I got up, went to the kitchen, poured a glass of tap water. I paced. I clutched the sink while the next contraction snaked its way up my pelvis to my low back. I inhaled and exhaled. I called the doctor. I trusted my doctor then. He told me to time the contractions. Drink the water. Lie down on my left side. Breathe.

I was walking from the kitchen to the living room to light the fire when a wet warmth filled my underwear and ran down my stockings. I waddled to the bedroom to strip off the wet clothes. Sitting on the toilet, hunched over in a spasm of pain, I struggled to remember the chemical equation for chloroform. It came to me as I looked down and saw a ribbon of deep maroon stain the toilet water.

I don't know what time it is, but the bottle is empty now. This was Thomas' favorite bottle. Not too peaty or smoky. Smooth. Opened with a drop of water. Single malt. Our anniversary bottle. It's our anniversary and I drink the last sips, reading the letter I got from Paul.

Dear Mrs. Dennis,

Can I call you Joan? My mother raised me to be respectful, but it feels strange to do that in a letter like this. Thank you for writing and your concern. You will be pleased to know that your house seems to be in good hands; the fields are mowed and the barn has been painted. I don't especially like the color, but to each his own. I was married. My wife died five years ago from cancer. We didn't have any children. I know you didn't ask that, but everyone always does. When I think of my grandmother, with six children, I wonder sometimes whether that was why we never found her. Maybe six was too many. I wanted to know, did you ever see anything in the house that was not yours? I ask only because my mother once told me that grandma kept a locked chest in her bedroom that none of the kids were allowed to get at. Why that would not have made it out, I don't know. I didn't know that your husband was in the Navy, by the way. I read his obituary in the paper. Please be well. And write any time.

Take care,
Paul

The hospital was so quiet. I'd thought it would be full of beeps and blips and rolling beds, nurses yelling, doctors rushing. Instead it was like walking in the woods after a heavy snow. I laid in the bed, propped up on pillows, waiting for Thomas. David had been blue. Unresponsive. His tiny fingers and toes perfect. Whole. Dead. It's painful giving birth to the dead. But I guess that's what women have done for millennia; everyone is born to die.

The woman I met at the coffee shop after yoga class inquired: Was I from here? It's something everyone does, because there are only two types of people who live in Pine Hills: people whose families go back four or five generations, and those who started coming here on vacation, renting ramshackle fishing cottages on the lake and then later building big, modern mansions and commuting down from Rochester on the weekends. The latter then retire from their jobs, buy the big cottages on the lake, and spend summers in Pine Hills. The former has babies and repopulate the town. They never really leave.

When we were dating, I went up to Thomas' college one weekend with my friend Marie. Thomas had a paper to write, but I didn't want to be alone. We sat together under the flickering fluorescent lights of the humanities library, between tall bookshelves that nearly reached to the ceiling. I spent most of my time in the physical sciences library; the air was different here. Thomas wrote longhand and flipped pages back and forth on a huge anthology. I scribbled on my notepad.

Chemical equations.

Moving to equations.

Moving to doodling a toy poodle with a fine haircut.

Then to simplicity: Thomas + Joanie forever in a heart.

To the heart: muscles, valves, arteries.

I got hungry around noon, and we walked down to the only diner on campus.

"Did you get a lot done?"

Thomas was wiping bright orange egg yolk off his plate with an end of toast. It dripped from his lips. He slurped it in.

"Mmm?"

"Your work."

He wiped his chin with a napkin and took a sip of coffee.

"Oh, yeah. That wasn't for class."

"What?"

"I mean it was work, but just not for class."

I ate a bowl of tomato soup, pale oyster crackers floating. A grilled cheese sandwich on white bread.

"I thought you had a paper due Monday."

"I do."

"Then what the hell are you doing instead?"

"It's nothing."

"Nothing."

"It's something, but not for class."

I let my soup spoon clatter on the plate underneath the bowl. I tore open another plastic package of crackers.

"What a waste of my time."

Thomas stopped in mid-bite. He put down his other piece of toast. He fixed me with one eye; his other was a bit bad, tilting softly to a space near my ears.

"Nothing is ever wasted, Joanie."

My high school chemistry teacher, Mr. Eisenberg, taught me to value my mind. And my height. He was a small man. I could reach the extra glass bottles and test tubes and equipment he kept on tall shelves around the lab. Now, I paint the ceiling molding in my new house and think how hard I would work if I were shorter.

Thomas stopped going to his workshop after David died. When he walked into the hospital that night, he sat on my bed and held my hand but did not look in my eyes. He was not allowed to see the baby. The baby (no one would say his name out loud, though I painstakingly watched the nurse write it down as I dictated) was not here anymore. He was in the morgue.

Thomas wore a suit with tie loosened, collar open, gray t-shirt peeking through. His hair was combed back from his forehead.

"Maybe it's for the best," he said to my hand.

His words dispersed into the room and I inhaled; I would breathe them for decades.

I was discharged and sent home to recuperate from what had been a very normal delivery. Aside from the dead baby. A month later, my mother and my Grandma McKenna drove down from Pine Hills and sat in my kitchen, waiting for something to happen. I baked a poppy seed cake drizzled with lemon glaze. I told them Darryl was staying on at the school, and that Thomas' factory was looking for a new director of research and development. Since I am tall, evidence of the baby was stretched out over expanses of skin and bone, disappearing faster than for any of the girls they knew my age back in Pine Hills.

"Speaking of your age," my mother said, "Have you talked to your doctor yet about when you're clear to try again?"

"We're not going to."

"Smart girl," said Grandma.

"Mother!"

"Jacqueline, please. It is not your life."

"But Mother, Joanie is still young!"

To me: "Joanie, please just ask. It can't hurt."

I crushed another piece of cake into my mouth.

"Thank you both, really, for your concern. But we've decided."

They spent a week in our house, arguing over whether I should work full-time or stay home to care for Thomas, who had become quieter, smaller, and sickly. But I was not going to stay home. Thomas would have to buck up.

I've gone through Boxes 1 and 2, and now I have the small chest in front of me and wonder: Do I jimmy it open with a crowbar? Why didn't I think of this sooner? Do I have a crowbar? The chest is so small, it's almost a joke. But it has a scrollwork lock and a tiny key hole. It's a decorative flair I now associate with Paul's grandmother, who had six children and walked off one day into the woods, never to be seen again. There was no key. I asked Thomas once to make one for me, but he laughed. Yet I stored the tiny chest in my woodland shed for years. I never opened it, but had never been able to throw it away.

Thomas spent a lot of time in the woods. He would come home from work with me midweek, during the spring and summer, strip out of his suit, and pull on his boots. The sun would be waning in the sky, and we'd walk into the woods beyond the gate and barn. One day, his pace was maniacal, practically running. My legs cramped up going over a fallen log, over a small hill, and then down into a valley. And then back up to the crest of another hill, suddenly opening onto a silent hall of tall, thin pine trees. The brown needles carpeting the ground muffled our footsteps.

Thomas disappeared around a large boulder atop the hill. I followed.

"Here!"

In a clearing, he stood on the doll-sized porch of a one-room shed. I could touch the roof's peak if I stood on tiptoes. We pried open the door barred by a piece of wood. Inside was a table and a three-legged stool. And a book that appeared rooted to the floor boards, its pages green and brown with mold, time, air.

"*Little Women.*"

I grab Thomas' hand and squeeze: "I've always wanted my own play house."

We laid back on the slightly slick floor, covered with a thin coating of moss, then peeled off our clothes. Our legs and arms were everywhere, out the window, out the front door. It was much better now that we didn't have to worry about pregnancy or death or both. Finally, sex was a divine act again.

The smell of pine still makes me wet, even now. Mr. Eisenberg said everything is relative. Grandma McKenna still thinks about Grandpa

Harold, she said, when she drinks a glass of orange juice with pulp; the pulpy bits pop in her mouth, she remembers the hard linoleum floor and the smell of burnt toast as she lay back, looking up at the ceiling and her new husband.

The dollhouse shed became my sanctuary and, sometimes, Thomas also went there alone. I brought in a reading chair, and Thomas ran a long wire from the barn to the shed, so I could have a lamp. I installed a tiny wood stove and pulled the small chest from the barn and placed it next to my chair.

Dear Joan,

I haven't heard from you in a while, are you okay? My wife used to say that no news is good news, but that doesn't always apply, does it? The weather here has been horrible. Warm enough for the trees to think it's spring, then that cold snap and frost and utter destruction. We have (had) a small orchard, but this year will be a bust. How is Sam? My dog Milo is lonely when I am at work. Any ideas how to keep him happy? They say, a dog with a bone... Joan, I meant to ask, are you taking visitors? I am coming up to the area in May, and wondered if you were around for coffee or lunch. I will understand if not. I'm not always up for company either.

Best,
Paul

P.S. Please don't feel bad about not writing. It took me three days to finish this letter...

I am sitting on the new floor, which is so damn shiny and slippery that my knees have slid out twice trying to get this thing open. I have used, in order: a flat head screwdriver, a Philip's head, a metal letter opener I found in the Keep box, and a can of black beans. My hands are cramping up. I'm going to take one last stab at this, because if I don't open this chest, I will take it to the curb outside my house and affix a FREE sign to it, and in less than a day, it will be gone. Someone will decide they need this castoff. I must open it or let it go. There's a hammer and mallet in Thomas' tool bag. He bought the hammer for $100. He told me it has special properties. I will put them to the test.

We stood near where the great Eastern white pine presided over the Garden of Serenity, under the green tent, waiting. The hole before us was just large enough to house the urn holding David's ashes; the urn weighed more than the ashes. The pine tree was decorated with metal windchimes that tinkled while we listened to people speaking. Thomas and I swayed with the windchimes. The urn was placed, the bronze headstone uncovered, flowers laid. The clean, green pine scent wafted over us and David, resting. To experience birth and death in one instant. I laid my head on Thomas' shoulder and vowed never to waste a thing again.

That's why I can't throw a goddamn thing away, why *he* can't throw a thing away. Why I spent three weeks pawing away at the piles of crap in the barn, the garage, the shed, the bonus room! Why I can't part with the stacks and piles and cardboard file boxes of his papers and scribbles. Why I can't read them. Why I spend an entire night staring at the boxes, willing them to rise and speak. Why I am obsessed with cracking opening this tiny chest. Sam nuzzles me then, licks my knuckles. I pat his head as reflex and realize I am alive. I grab the hammer and mallet, align them over the lock, poise my entire height and weight above it, and let it rain down. WHACK! Again. CLANG! Again. CA-CHUNK!

The lock cracks. I am sweating. I open the chest with my big hands; inside, there is a single slip of crumpled paper. It's a receipt from the store the chest was bought in. 1935.

&

Paul is wearing the same boots and, maybe, the same mud on them. He is smiling. His face is luminous with sun reflected off the lake.

"This is amazing."

"I know."

"Do you wanna eat now?"

I hadn't been to the diner in town since high school. It looked the same, all chrome and faded red leather seats. We ordered coffee and I told Paul I'd made a new friend at yoga class.

"She's so cute. Wants to introduce me to her old mother-in-law!"

He chuckles while reading the menu.

"She could be my daughter."

It is something I think about.

Paul orders a tuna melt on rye. A Coke. A slice of apple pie for dessert. He's a man with appetite. He's a good head shorter than I am.

"What do you want to do while you're here?"

"Not much."

"We can walk by the outlet. Or I know this place we can walk to a waterfall."

"Okay, let's do that."

I order the tomato soup with crackers and grilled cheese.

"What do you do again, Paul?"

I don't know him as I should.

"Appliance repair."

It's a throw-away answer, and he's looking at me. His eyes crinkle at the edges. I put my hand on the table between us.

"Can you fix my new stove? It's not working right."

"Sure. I'll take look at it. Later though."

Yes, no time to waste. The sun is out today.

William Connor

Ice Power
Patricia Owen

Winter can come fierce and cold in the Finger Lakes of New York. The power of moving ice can't be ignored, so people living along the lake's shore take out docks, swim float platforms, and boat hoists every year. They take everything out in the fall, and put it all back in the spring or early summer. Those are lake rituals.

We purchased a small but old cottage and began learning its history. In the lowest level where we stored oars, paddles, life jackets, and even a small kayak, the previous owners had written the date each year when they put the dock back in. "I wonder if we can brave the icy cold water and put it in before they ever did," my husband said under his breath one day.

On St. Patrick's Day, Jim and our kindergartner granddaughter put in the dock. There was still ice on the lake about a mile north. They wrote the date along side those later dates on the ceiling beam.

After completing the task, they walked up along the shore and broke off a piece of ice to watch it move by slight wind and wave action toward the south. Sarah even stepped onto that piece of ice to ride it, just one or two feet from shore. Soon it began to melt, and she jumped off.

That was such fun they broke off another chunk, but it floated south a bit too far out for Sarah to ride it. She and her granddad played Jarts with the flat ice float and stones. It was great fun to see how many stones each could throw onto the ice. They watched until that piece of ice also melted out in the lake.

They went back to break off another piece. Jim pushed with a stick over and over, and finally a piece broke loose and started moving south, faster than the other two. This third piece was not a small round slab. It was about 800 feet long by our guestimate.

I'd returned home from work in time to see the mischief those two were getting into. By the time I changed clothes, Jim was in waders, trying to figure out how to keep the huge piece of ice from ramming our dock and bending it to pieces. The ice was coming fast.

Jim got a long board and went along the shore trying to push the ice flow farther out. It was clear that he was not in charge of its speed or direction. The ice didn't appear to be getting smaller as night fell and the temperature dropped significantly. We started to plan. Perhaps we could push together. Perhaps we could stand one hour shifts, pushing it out all night.

Meanwhile, the ice came closer and closer. Finally its edge was just at our dock. Jim strongly nudged the front edge of the ice out past our dock. Whew! Then he pushed from a point farther along. And then again and again. The huge piece of ice looked like it might pass the end of our dock. But it didn't. Jim pushed several more times. Each time it went out a little farther, and each time it came back in a little faster.

It didn't pass us by, and it wasn't getting any smaller. The forward edge ran aground on the shore just south of our dock. Now what? Jim pushed it out. The wind pushed it back. He pushed out. And back in it came, right toward the dock.

I was ready to practice my hourly shift, even with my hands freezing cold. I could see Sarah's concerned little face at the cottage window. She turned right as it went out, and she turned left as it came back. I took a turn pushing out with all my might, trying not to fall in the icy lake. This was hard. I had pushed about four times, and I was ready to give the task back to Jim. He took a turn of twelve hearty pushes. Then he stepped out of the water to breathe. His respite was cut short, because the ice was heading in once again, and faster this time.

It was a starless night, very cold and very dark. The ice was coming back in. I was sure we would lose the dock of pipes held with heavy metal sleeves and wooden sections. I wondered how Jim and his pint-sized helper got the dock in by themselves. I knew from some of their other adventures that all Jim needed was a little bit of help for his engineering feats. Of course, he had done most of the work. Sarah had probably held the wrench, handed the bolts, and perhaps handed him some of the lighter pipes.

Suddenly, I was jolted out of my reverie by seeing Jim wading as deep as he could go into the lake with his chest-high waders. I didn't want him to fall and fill those high boots full of ice water. I stiffened as I watched, and held my breath.

Jim breathed several heavy breaths and pushed with all his strength. The ice went out away from our dock. It went a little farther than before. It went out a little farther, and the water and wind caught it and pushed it along. Then it cartwheeled around, coming away from its grounding at the shore.

We saw the forward end coming around toward us and gasped, but it came around enough to the south to miss us.

With energy spent and our pent-up tenseness released, we laughed a giddy laugh and hugged each other in bear hugs.

We tugged off our wet mittens and gear and had giant mugs of hot chocolate with pancakes for dinner.

Happy St. Patrick's Day. We vowed never to try to beat the record, and always to wait until all the ice is *out*.

Robin Farley

If You Listen Very Hard
Bethany Snyder

No one was sure how long the cop had been standing there, leaning against the car and watching us. Ally swore later that she saw a glint of light off his badge, but more likely it was that we finally stopped laughing long enough to hear the motor of his car running.

By then we were all sprawled out on the grass, and I was trying to count the stars. The lights in the parking lot made it impossible to see more than the brightest ones. Will's shoulder was pressed up against mine, his skin sweet with chlorine and cologne. He and Johnny had gone in the pool, peeled off their t-shirts and dropped their jeans, slipping into the blue water in just their boxers. I never saw anything more beautiful in my life than him walking up to me after, dripping wet with a *look what I got away with* grin.

I thought maybe this would be the night we kissed. Maybe right then, laying in the grass with a little buzz from the beers and just enough shadow to make it feel like we were alone. Then the cop cleared his throat and asked us what we thought we were doing there. Johnny answered, "Trespassing, officer," very serious and respectfully. That made the cop laugh. We all knew him, or of him anyway, a star on the football team before he broke his shoulder. His little sister was in my Algebra II class. He told us to get our stuff and get gone, and to not make a habit of entering state parks after hours.

Will always wanted to drive my car. I always let him. He was big enough that he had to cram his knees against the dashboard. He wasn't much taller than Johnny, but everything about him seemed big. Like he had outgrown himself, his life, our town. He was too big for me to hold on to, but I tried.

I thought we would go back into town, maybe get some pizza, but instead Will turned left out of the park. "Not the chapel," Ally said, quiet but serious, in the back seat. I could hear the shiver in her voice.

"Never the chapel," Will said. He nudged me with his elbow and my skin grew warm, like it would glow in the dark. He turned off the main road, and soon we were on dirt and gravel, winding up and up, deep into the Bluff. We passed the chapel, a dark shadow along the treeline.

The radio was on, low, and Will sang along under his breath. The one time we danced, late on prom night, he sang all the wrong words to "Stairway to Heaven" into a spot just under my ear. My fingers slipped in the sweat on the back of his neck, and he crushed the mint-green silk of my dress when he pressed me closer. It was the happiest eight minutes of my life, until tonight.

He parked in the long grass at the side of the road. We listened to the *tick tick* of the engine. "Come on," Will said after a minute, and opened his door. Johnny and Ally were quiet in the backseat, except the rustle of clothes.

There was no moon, and the trees closed in around us, hardly enough room to get past the car. "I can't see anything," I said. The dark was like a living thing around me, closing in. I didn't want to keep walking. What was out there in the black? Then I heard Will come up in front of me. I put out my hand and touched his chest, his t-shirt still damp from the swim. I wanted to hold on to him, to see how much of him I could get my arms around, but I just held on to his shirt instead.

"I'm here," he said. He took my hand, interlaced our fingers, and pulled me along through the black. I felt hot, like a red ember in a campfire.

"What's out here?"

He told me to hush, so I did. We walked under a tight canopy of trees, just him and me and ten thousand crickets, the underbrush tickling my ankles. I stayed as close to Will as I could without tripping him or me. We were breathing at the same time, quick and shallow. Finally, when I thought we would walk right off the bluff and fall into the lake, we stopped.

"Here, sit," he said. He pulled my hand down and to the left, and there was old, smooth wood—a log on its side. I sat, and Will sat next to me, close. I wanted to say things to him, the secrets about him that I held in my heart, but I didn't know how to make the words come.

He put a finger under my chin and lifted it up. The trees opened up over our heads, a perfect circle of sky. I couldn't count those stars, not in a hundred lifetimes. Will settled, his body warm and close. He talked then, about finals and the Navy and his dad, about lacrosse and David Bowie and buying a truck. The whole time I just looked up at the sky. The harder I looked, the more stars I saw.

"Are you listening?" he said, loud but not mad. He leaned into me, pressed himself right up along my side. I wondered if he felt fire running under his skin, too.

"I'm always listening," I said back.

I could see his teeth in the dark. The biggest smile. "Ah, look!"

All around us were lightning bugs, blinking green and bright, like the stars had fallen out of the sky to be near us. We sat very still, and they flew close to our faces, landed on our hands and knees.

"I'm never going to forget this," Will said, showing me the little bug on his fingertip. I swallowed hard. This was the time for the kiss, the perfect time. I'd tell my granddaughters about this kiss, when their damp hair was set in braids and they were snug in their little beds. Will would have a beard and a pipe, probably, and doze off in his chair after dinner.

But he just put his arm around me and looked back up at the sky. I glowed hot and feverish where his skin touched mine, burned bright as the lightning bugs, brighter than the stars. I wanted to stay there all night, wait for the sun to come up and break through the trees and light the face of this boy who set me on fire.

By the end of the next year, Will would be gone, lost to all of us. For now, though, it was just him and me and the stars wheeling overhead, and the possibility of everything, spinning out in front of us, forever.

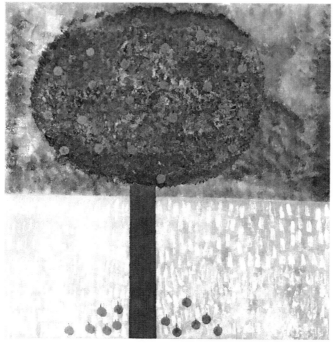

Teresa Tomion

Every Morning He Says To Me "Seven"
Ben Baker

Every morning he says to me "seven," in the language that we use. Long ago it was decided that, out of ten, seven was the best kind of love—not too hot, not too cold. On mornings when I wake up without him, I look squarely in the mirror and try to say "seven" to myself.

We have our betty lives together, in our little town. It's not so bad.

Down the stairs in the nearly-light, him in front of me, I ask what he wants for breakfast. "Just crunch" is plain cereal. "Squares" are the frozen waffles, forty to a box, that we eat in fits and starts some

117

months. The language that we use.

I notice the way he organizes things, even if he doesn't mean me to. The dishes, dry, just so, or our jackets in the closet. If we had a housekeeper, I could tell their works apart.

When he leaves to job, I watch him back Matilda, smoking smoke, from the driveway, waving vertically, with invisible worried hanky, as if from the deck of a ship. I wave back from the quay. He is a great intrepid, my him, and a mighty traveler.

Each thing has a name, and, alone, I name them for nobody. This thing, this universal shape, is called chair. This chair is called Oscar, for its color and shag, this one Sit Upon, for the Girl Scouts. All of these, all stacked and bellied up, are called rooms. This room is called Jupiter, for no reason.

On days when I don't job, I walk. I take provisions seriously. A backpack is a kind of a thing that holds everything you need. And then some. And now some. Already heavy, magazine heavy, *New Yorker* heavy, it takes food and water both, food that I love but still call "yuck," because he calls it that. Fully watered and yucked, I walk.

I pack the paper and glance at the headlines, wonder who else might know the same news as me. Along the way, I touch a telephone pole, third up the block, in the same place every time. That place is smooth, and oily, as if it has been touched by many hands before mine. If there's another body on the block, I nod at the pole in our private way.

Town is just a town without its folks, and we know each other well. Tom who bikes and Sarah who has Smelly on a chain and Heavy Metal Mango, who sits on his roof with the music too loud and throws horns at us whatever the weather.

To love is to know shortcuts, and I love my town. Every street has a song, every alley a hum. Here I was with him, early on. Here I found a cat I couldn't help.

To love is know landmarks. Here is where the county sits. Here a record was broken with buckwheat.

On the trail are people I already don't know. I wonder where they come from, their countries and communities, the rules they have for their children, the language that they use. Footstep, footstep, hoofclop, chainsqueak, a scurrying perpendicular to the path.

Where the way is empty, I fancy myself the last one standing, the survivor. I have me, I have my wits. I don't miss my him, I don't think, and I don't think I don't mind. And then there are the families and the farmers and the laughing girls and all of that again.

He had thought once to rent us a canoe that we launched in the outlet, downstream, towards the lake that we met on. Under bridge and past mill we wobbled, unaware of our instability, until we dumped it on a snag. We panicked, counting heads and arguing the finer points of marine salvage: nobody told us that canoes didn't sink. All that was lost was one sorry sandal, a prize for some snapping turtle.

Here and there, I walk though the cold patches that I learned from Scout were called "haints." The word feels strange in my mouth, so I don't call them anything at all.

Home again, the floors lie like open fields in the afternoon, almost as if someone had been cleaning up. That old housekeeper. I laze, I laze, I laze, nipping and pawing like cat until I get self-conscious in the empty room.

When he returns, he lifts from his shoes in the hall, last steps preserved. "Where do the pennies even go?" he asked, when he got those job shoes, as if I would have known.

We talk about the people that he met. "How were their stairs?" I ask, to tease. He fancied himself an architect when we were young, when we were all neon for each other, full ten. He knows about houses, lectures me on their designs, always defined by the stairs. I had no idea. "Colonial," he'll say, about a client, centered. Or "ranch," nothing doing. "Split-level," he'll say, shallow. Or "raised ranch."

Straight-up. Get it?

He has yet, to my knowledge, to meet a mansion.

We have a picture, not of us, not of anything, framed in magnets. Treetops and a bit of cloud, a missnapped shot from early on. We were walking on the Bluff, finger on the shutter. "Aspirations of the Day," he calls it. As far as I know, he doesn't have names for any other pictures.

After dinner, we spin a one or two, a side-to-side, and read the liner notes. Familiar names appear and appear. John did Leon. Rob did Richard. Coincidences kill me. The language that we use.

It's funny how he sits, with a beer or a book or a screen, unaware of his own body. If I were in that body, I would be aware of all the sitting I did strangely.

I gave him, once, a dictionary, small and pocket-sized with type to match. I told him I had circled important words, but I just liked to watch him hunt. I described him later as "fossiliferous" and went to circle it, but it wasn't there. I added my best definition in pocket-sized print.

Sometimes, before all the lights are on, around a corner startles me. "What are you so scared of?" I hear from him. He calls me Little Rabbit or Jumpy G, neither of which I like.

Today, I'm scared of getting old in a high-rise, with a stupid dog whose tongue curls back into its own nose, and who I love so much that I not only find a voice for it, but it a voice for me. I don't tell him that.

Up the stairs in the nearly-dark, him in front of me, we creak more towards the top. Colonial. In the bathroom is a jar to hold our toothbrushes, the very same jar that held the brushes in his apartment. Still cute, just cleaner now.

As we shine our pearls, he leans into the wall, or into me. Out the window, the neighborhood goes soft around the edges. A car moves slowly. A garbage can rolls. An owl. I like that.

He gets ready, fast or slow, and flops, and reads with the lamp over his shoulder. I read, sometimes, or debate with him, or roll my body towards the wall. And then we sleep, almost not touching, and every morning he says to me "seven."

About the Authors

ALEX ANDRASIK is originally from Fredonia, New York. In Yates County, he is active in LGBTQ advocacy, the promotion of literacy and the arts, and political and civic action. As Director of Adult Services at the Penn Yan Public Library, he facilitates public programs that entertain, educate, and inform.

BEN BAKER is a writer, musician, and educator living in Rochester, where he enjoys long paddles, bike commuting, and cold beverages. Ben is proficient in animal husbandry, moving silently, hats, and detecting missing hyphens.

SINGER BARDIN is originally from Louisiana, but now spends most of his time around Steuben County and NYC. He is an active player on social media, and can be found on Facebook and Twitter. His favorite things are puppy breath, the color green, and eating his weight in cheese.

BUTCH BURRIS was born in Rochester, and lived on Keuka Lake and in Penn Yan. He received an AAS degree from Alfred Tech, and served in the Navy for twenty years. Now retired, he teaches knitting, crochet, and guitar. He and his wife, Annie, live in Albany.

LISA CAVANAUGH is a fourth generation Keuka Lake resident. She adores all things Finger Lakes, especially drinking the wine, putting along in her father's wooden boats, and photographing the amazing landscapes. She and her husband Pete are raising another generation of Lake rat kids: Brianna, Lizzie, Maddie, and Owen.

DEBBIE KOOP is from Rochester, but spent childhood summers at Keuka Lake. Her career in the organic food industry spanned retailer, wholesaler, broker, distributor, manufacturer. In 1993, Debbie and her husband, Len Saner, bought historic Brookside Farm to raise grass fed, organic beef cattle.

R. MURPHY is the pseudonym of a crabby—yet shy and retiring—woman of a certain age who had the privilege of living on Keuka's shores for a number of years while she penned the Bob books: *Bob at the Lake, Bob at The Plaza,* and *Bob and the Polka-Dot Highway.*

PATRICIA OWEN writes brochures, study materials, voice overs, and more. Her writing reflects her New Jersey childhood, New England to Rochester, then home in Penn Yan. She always has a pen in hand. She has written two novels, and is researching Glenn Curtiss, caregivers, and global places - New York names.

MERRILL LAURA (BROWN) RACE is a lifelong resident of Penn Yan, a graduate of Finger Lakes Community College, and a retired early childhood education teacher. She is an active member of the Yates County History Center. She lives along the shores of Keuka Lake with her family and two cats.

BETHANY SNYDER is a voice-over artist, an amateur photographer, a cookie connoisseur, a Maine enthusiast, a horror movie aficionado, and a pop-culture junkie who loves the sea and semi-colons. She works as the Creative Director for an online learning company, and writes fiction from her home in Penn Yan.

P.T. SWEENEY is writer and editor. A native of Penn Yan, he is a graduate of St. Bonaventure University, and now lives in Massachusetts with his wife and daughter.

SARAH THOMPSON writes, teaches yoga, and grows grapes in Penn Yan, on the western shores of Seneca Lake. She's written for Cornell University, *Edible Finger Lakes, Finger Lakes Wine Country* magazine, and is author of *Finger Lakes Wine Country* (Arcadia Press, 2015). Her favorite Finger Lakes season is fall.

R.W. WEBB is a lifetime writer from rural North Carolina who currently lives in Penn Yan. His work has appeared in *Bewildering Stories, Bleeding Ink Anthology, Deep South Magazine, McSweeney's,* and more. He fell in love with the Finger Lakes fifteen years ago, and has no intention of leaving.

BRUCE WESTERDAHL worked as a college administrator and lay pastor. He wrote a column in the *Chronicle Express* as the Old Grape Stomper from 1995-1996. Currently, he blogs at *Contemporary Parables*. He and his wife, Nancy, also blog about their experiences *Growing Up in Gettysburg in the Forties.*

ALEXANDER WORTHAM grew up in New Jersey, spent time overseas when he was young, and attended college in Buffalo. He's been visiting the Finger Lakes since the late 90s, and lived on Keuka Lake after college, where he met his wife. He lives in Rochester, where he works in banking.

About the Artists

Bluff & Vine is thrilled to feature art from SkylArc Studio in Penn Yan. SkylArc is a day services program that provides opportunities for individuals with developmental disabilities to express themselves through art.

SkylArc artists work in the mediums of glass mosaics, acrylics, paper mache, photography, glass fusing, pottery, and printmaking.

Members of the studio are always pleased to welcome visitors, and are proud to showcase their artistry. SkylArc operates out of the Arc of Yates facility on North Ave in Penn Yan.

Visit the online gallery at *bluffandvine.com* to view the artwork featured in this volume in beautiful color, information on which pieces are for sale, and how you can purchase them.

CPSIA information can be obtained
at www.ICGtesting.com
Printed in the USA
LVOW12s1507051217
558726LV00002B/506/P

9 781979 408257